Susan Kowick

W9-BHF-315

It Takes Two
to Talk

Ayala Manolson

The
Hanen
Program®

A HANEN CENTRE PUBLICATION

The
Hanen
Program®

A HANEN CENTRE PUBLICATION
Copyright 1992

All rights reserved. No part of this book may be
produced by mimeograph or by any other means
without the written permission of the publisher.
Excerpts may be printed in connection with
published reviews in periodicals without express
permission.

Copies of the book may be ordered from the
publisher: **THE HANEN CENTRE,**
               1075 Bay Street, Suite 403
               Toronto, Ontario CANADA M5S 2B1
               (416) 921-1073 Fax (416) 921-1225
               E-mail: info @ hanen.org
               World Wide Web: http://www.hanen.org

Third Revision, 1992

National Library of Canada
ISBN 0-921145-02-0

Table of Contents

We all have a dream, we all have a hope, we all have an expectation that one day our child will learn to talk, naturally and effectively. But learning to talk means much more than learning the right words. It means learning to recognize feelings. It means learning to understand thoughts. It means learning to be a person, and how to connect with another person.

A child doesn't learn to communicate by himself. He learns through involvement with his world. We, his parents, are the largest part of that world, and it's what we do and how we do it that affects our child's opportunities to learn. It takes two to talk.

Acknowledgements

Changes in the 1992 revision are based on the insightful recommendations given by dedicated speech-language pathologists across Canada, the U.S.A., Portugal and Israel who have used this guide book in their Hanen parent programs. Their input was invaluable.

This revision also includes changes suggested by my committed and capable colleagues Claire Watson and Elaine Weitzman, arising from their use of the guide book with our parent groups at the Hanen Centre in Toronto.

There can be no full accounting of my debt to the thousands of parents and children whose participation in Hanen language programs has contributed to development of this approach since its inception in 1975. They know who they are and will recognize their input here and there. To them my thanks.

Having experts from diversified fields co-operate toward the common goal of communication has greatly enriched this book. To my daughters Ilana and Frith, my gratitude and thanks for sharing their expertise as creative artists and mothers of young children. Their experiences significantly enrich Chapter 8, "Creating Together." I'm grateful to Maria Martella for compiling the book resource list for Chapter 7.

The many drafts of this revision have been considerably improved by input from: my dear friend Helen Buck; writer, broadcaster, and Hanen parent Richard Ouzonian; and my wonderful and demanding husband Will Manolson. Hugh Oliver provided meticulous copy editing. The chapter "Creating Together" is in large part the writing of Ilana Manolson and Susan Klein.

My heartfelt admiration and appreciation to Jerry Newton, whose talent as a graphic artist made the information come alive on the page, and to Ruth Ohi, whose delightful illustrations make you smile while you learn. I would also like to thank Ilana Manolson, whose drawings in the 1985 edition of "It Takes Two to Talk" inspired many of the new illustrations.

Throughout the process, the support of the Hanen office staff has been indefatigable: Tom Khan who has admirably handled the problem of delay in publication by mailing out hundreds of drafts, and Adele Ritchie and Katie Hrycyk for typing and retyping variations on the theme.

I should also like to mention my enormous debt to The Ontario Ministry of Community and Social Services and to my supervisors Faith Mills and Frank Cummings. Over the last 10 years, they have provided me with financial support and encouragement to establish a model parent program in early language intervention. This revision of "It Takes Two to Talk" has also been make possible through their funding.

Disappointed and frustrated by our child's limited desire or ability to communicate with us, we may feel like giving up or giving in just to put an end to it. However, not only will we lose, but our child will not have the opportunity or encouragement he needs to improve his ability to communicate and learn.

The Hanen Approach is counter-intuitive for most of us because it requires us to do the opposite of what we might naturally do when communication breaks down. The essence of this approach is to encourage communication by indirect action. We go around our child's resistance. Rather than telling him what to do, we let him figure it out. We make it easier for our child to enjoy the pleasures and benefits of communicating.

This approach focuses on the caring connections that help our children communicate and learn. It is called the **3a Way**. It reminds us to:

allow our child to lead

adapt to "share the moment"

add language and experience.

The **3a Way** to encourage communication can be used with all children — with an ill infant, a hostile toddler, a temperamental preschooler. It is a helpful approach that anyone can use to encourage communication.

For parents of children who are at risk of becoming or are already identified as language-delayed, the information in this book can best be supported by their involvement in a Hanen Parent Training Program. This program further enriches and individualizes the Hanen Approach to meet the family's needs. The quality of the program is assured by the certification of Hanen-trained speech-language pathologists.

Ayala Manolson

Introduction

The greatest gift we can give a child is help in learning to communicate and connect with his world, but each of us has had to face the frustration and discomfort of trying to communicate with a child who is unable, uninterested or impossible to understand. Under stress, even caring, reasonable parents can become frustrated and angry, and even turn into screaming maniacs. Communication with our children can bog down or break down, consuming our time, our energy, and even worse leaving us feeling ineffective.

These kinds of situations call for more than ordinary communication skills. How do we talk to a child who has a limited ability to communicate? A child who doesn't want to communicate? A child who won't listen? A child who is constantly on the move? A child who lets you know "My way or no way"?

This book lays out an approach to overcome these barriers to good communication — our child's limited ability to communicate, his negative emotions, his perceived lack of power, his skepticism about the benefits of communicating.

Our child may fail to communicate not because he is uninterested but because he is unsure of how to respond. Even if our child has the ability to respond he may feel that he will not be understood and so reject communicating. Further, our child's response may appear unreasonable because he knows no other way of communicating. He is merely using the skills he has. Behind our child's behaviour may lie fear or distrust. He may not respond as a way of protecting or defending himself.

The problem we are up against is not only our child's behaviour but also our own reaction to our child's behaviour. When our child appears disinterested we are inclined to take over or withdraw. When he rejects our efforts to communicate with him we are inclined to retaliate with direct pressure. When he insists on his position we want to reject it and assert our own. In trying to break down our child's resistance, we usually increase it.

CHAPTER ONE

Allow Your Child to Lead

"I believe the children are our future.
Teach them well, and let them lead the way,
Show them all the beauty they possess inside,
Give them a sense of pride to make it easier,
Let the children's laughter remind us how we used to be..."

Linda Creed, songwriter

This chapter is about:

- being willing to allow our children to lead so they have the chance to express their feelings, needs and interests.

- how we affect our children's opportunities to gain a sense of pride and feel the beauty they possess inside.

- getting to know our children by taking the time to discover, wait for and listen to their attempts to communicate.

- knowing what to expect from our children.

You Make the Difference

*As parents, we play many roles ... sometimes all at once.
We have to be a policeman who tries to be a pal, a storyteller
who doubles as chauffeur, and a diaper changer who specializes
in damage control.*

*Sometimes we forget that how we play these parts affects
the opportunities that our child has to learn. We forget
that **how** we do **what** we do makes a difference.*

When we play "The Helper"

We want to be good parents. We want to be there whenever we think our child wants or needs something. It's hard to resist this natural instinct to make everything simpler, easier, faster and clearer by saying it or doing it for our child when he seems unable to say it or do it for himself.

However, what seems simpler, easier and more helpful today deprives our child of the chances he needs to express his curiosity, feelings and needs. When we do and say everything for our child, **we deny him the chance to learn by trying or saying it for himself.**

*"Don't trouble dear,
I'll do it for you."*

"I've got so much to do, I've got to move."

When we play "The Mover"

We have so much to do. The planning, the scheduling, the working, the shopping, the organizing, the doing, the coming and going ... all these things will surely help our child have a richer, fuller, happier day-to-day life.

The problem is that trying to do everything can take up so much of our time and energy that our child gets lost in the shuffle.

If we have something scheduled for every minute of every day, chances are that the schedule doesn't allow us time to make the caring connection with our child that will help him learn. **We find ourselves talking at our child rather than with him.**

When we play "The Teacher"

We know that as parents our job is to teach, and we have so much to teach our child that we often find ourselves doing most of the talking.

We too often forget that our child learns best by doing, rather than watching or being told what to do and how to do it. **When we do most of the talking, our child doesn't get a chance to learn by doing.**

"Now listen to me. I'll teach you what to do."

"If I listen to you, then you'll listen to me."

When we play "The Responsive Partner"

We use the **3a** Way to encourage our child to connect and communicate. Our child feels recognized and special because we:

allow our child to lead us

adapt to share the moment

add language and experience

Our undivided attention and our warm responsiveness to our child's attempts to communicate help him develop feelings of self-confidence, power, and satisfaction.

When we take the time to share experiences with our child, **it encourages him to make the human connections that will help him learn.**

It Takes Two to Talk ... and what we do makes the difference. It's hard to help our child learn to talk when we're busy doing everything for him, constantly on the move, or focused on teaching. Being a responsive partner will give us limitless opportunities to talk with our child and help him learn.

Know Your Child Intimately

> "I will know you.
> I will touch you and hold you.
> And smell and taste and listen
> To the noises that you make ... and the words if any.
>
> And then, when I have come to know you, intimately,
> I will insist, gently, gradually, but insist
> That you know me
> And later, that you trust me
> And then yourself.
> Now knowing each other, we will begin to know the world."
>
> *Mary MacCracken, teacher and author*

As Mary MacCracken so poetically reminds us, helping our child get to know the world begins with getting to know our child and gaining her trust.

In our desire to care for, to teach and to entertain our child, our natural instinct is to take over. It takes a conscious effort not to anticipate quickly what our child needs, not to tell her what to do, not to choose her play activities. It requires a conscious effort to take a moment, often it's only a few seconds, to **Observe, Wait and Listen** to our child.

Taking the time to:
> **Observe** — helps us recognize our child's feelings and needs
> **Wait** — gives our child a chance to express herself in her own way
> **Listen** — encourages our child to express herself.

These three very important words can be remembered by their first letters, **OWL:**

Observe

Wait and

Listen

Taking the time to **OWL** is the wise way to start.
Consciously taking the time to **OWL** is the first and most important step in getting to know our child intimately.

Observe

*As parents, our care and concern for our children and the time
we spend with them give us endless opportunities to observe
them carefully and get to know and understand them better.*

Even when our children don't use words, we
can easily recognize their **feelings or needs**
when we take the time to observe their:
- focus of attention
- facial expression
- body language

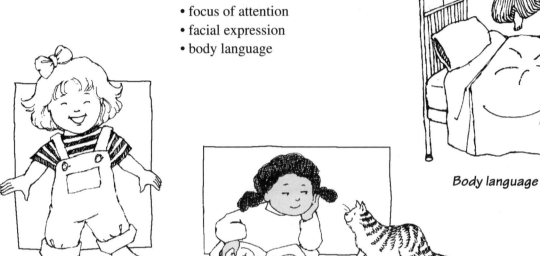

Body language

Facial expression

Focus of attention

But sometimes our children's facial expressions, actions and focus of attention
are not clear enough to help us figure out what they are trying to tell us.
Observing the following subtle cues can be helpful:

- state of alertness
- rate of breathing
- change in skin tone
- the pitch, volume, and duration of their sounds

*It takes time and determination to get to know the unique combination of
body language and sounds that each child uses to communicate.*

Wait

When we wait, we give our child the time he needs to express his interests and feelings in his own way.

Waiting for our child to communicate is hard to do!

Our lives keep moving at an increasingly rapid pace, and we have come to feel that a silent moment is an empty moment. As adults, we also feel that it's our duty to teach, test our child's knowledge, and conduct conversation. And so we tend not to wait for our child to express himself. Instead, we try to help in our own adult ways. We talk for our child, answer for our child, and use controlling language (commands and questions).

Taking over is a natural, even instinctive, reaction on our part. However, if we want to help our child learn, we must give him a chance to express himself in his own way.

If we make everything simpler, easier, and faster for ourselves, we may find that we're ignoring the feelings, needs, and curiosity of the child we care for and are concerned about.

Waiting gives us the chance to get to know our child. We can watch for his focus of attention, look at the expression on his face, and listen to the sounds he makes.

Listen

Are you listening to the music, Tyler? Is it nice music? Good. Nice music Good boy.

Sound familiar? How many times do we have a conversation with our child where we do all the talking?

When we talk and our child doesn't respond easily, our natural reaction is to fill in all the blanks, answer all the questions, and even comment without leaving a pause.

We think we're making things easier, but we're actually involved in a form of loving sabotage. We don't expect an answer, and our child usually fulfills our expectations by not communicating.

If we listen attentively to our child, our undivided attention will give our child the security and encouragement to make his efforts worthwhile.

If we listen attentively to our child, we will also understand him better and be able to respond more sensitively to him.

"The only way to know where a kid is 'at', is to listen to what he is saying. You can't do this if you are talking."

— Neil Postman and Charles Weingartner, educators

OWLing makes the difference

The pace of our busy lives and the expectations we have for our children often interfere with our ability to Observe, Wait and Listen sensitively to them.

Sometimes we need to consciously make the effort to OWL, to become more aware of our children's feelings, needs and interests. Laya, Ben and Katie's parents found that OWLing can make a difference.

Mom held Laya up to the mirror so she could see what a beautiful girl she was. Mom kept tapping the mirror to get her interest. But Laya kept bending her head down. Mom was puzzled that Laya wasn't as fascinated with the mirror as she thought she would be. When she noticed that Laya was looking at the flowers below the mirror, she followed her lead, and they had a great time smelling the roses!

Dad was trying to read a story to Ben. He read the words slowly and with animation in his voice, but Ben kept trying to turn the page. Dad soon realized that Ben wasn't interested in his story, and so he stopped reading. Then he noticed that Ben seemed fascinated with the picture of a big brown dog on the page. Dad started to bark, and then the fun began!

Katie was excited when she came home from a trip to the zoo, and began to tell her mom all about it. Mom interrupted and said, "Oh, did you like the monkeys?" Not waiting for Katie to answer, she went on, "I knew you would! They're my favorites too! Come on Katie, it's time to wash our hands for lunch." Katie's excitement was gone. She became sad and quiet. Mom forgot to OWL and missed a chance to talk with Katie about what had been most exciting for her — the popcorn!

If we find ourselves...

- *doing all the talking*
- *helping when it's not needed*
- *directing the show*
- *interrupting*
- *assuming that we know what our child wants to say*

... let's remember to take the time to OBSERVE, WAIT AND LISTEN to our children.

How You Can Allow Your Child to Lead — in Everyday Life

When milk spills,
we want to wipe it up right away...

but...

if we allow our child to lead, he will let us
know what he thinks about the situation.

- When the doorbell rings, we want to answer it immediately.
  But if we allow our child to lead, we will see if and how our child reacts to the sound.

- When we want to read a book to our child, we want to read it from cover to cover, exactly as it's written.
  But if we allow our child to lead, he will let us know what really interests him in the book.

- When our child tries to tell us something, we want to learn the information as quickly as possible and so we complete his sentences.
  But if we allow our child to lead, we learn what he's really trying to tell us.

- When we give our child a toy, we want him to play with the one we choose.
  But if we allow our child a choice, we will know what toy he wants to play with.

Communication Develops Gradually

Every child's ability to communicate develops gradually, and it's important to remember that each child develops at her own speed and in her own way. Children progress through five levels as they master the communication game.

Being aware of where our children are in their development will help us recognize and accept the way they are now communicating and what we can do to help them progress.

In the beginning, at **Level I**, our children, like **Laya,** make their interests and their needs known through their body language and the cooing and burbling sounds they make. As parents, we interpret their sounds and actions as communication.

At Level I, we can expect:
• cries • looks • smiles • screams
• vowel-like sounds
• changes in voice (loudness, etc.)
• changes in skin tone
• movement of body

Then, at **Level II**, our children, like **Ben**, take a great deal of joy in all the discoveries they make. They become interested in the people and things that enter their ever-expanding world. As they continue to experience, grow, and explore, their facial expressions and their gestures are easier for us to understand.

At Level II, we can expect:
• facial expressions
• movement toward objects and/or persons
• variety of consonant and vowel sounds
• ability to focus on objects and/or persons

At **Level III**, our children's communication skills increase, and like **Tyler**, they are able to connect and interact more easily with us. They direct more and more of their efforts toward trying to get our attention, help, or approval. They also begin to look to us for information.

At Level III, we can expect:
• pointing at specific objects or persons
• nodding and waving
• acting out what they mean
• making sounds that stand for words
• occasionally using single words/signs
• combining eye gaze, vocalization and gestures

At **Level IV**, our children, like **Katie**, begin to use words and/ or signs consistently. Their body language and facial expressions still help us to interpret their feelings.

At Level IV, we can expect:
• frequent use of single words/signs
• combinations of words which may be difficult for us to understand
• combinations of two or more words/signs in phrases or sentences

Then, at **Level V**, our children begin to combine three or more words into sentences. The information in this book focuses on helping children progress to Level V.

The developmental checklists at the back of this book will help you learn what level your child is at and give you detailed information about what you can expect your child to do next.

11

In summary,

when we **allow** our child to lead:

		our child
by **observing** our child's focus of attention, facial expressions and body language	→	• gives us the information we need to interpret and understand his feelings and interests

		our child
by **waiting** to give our child time to express himself	→	• has the opportunity to express his needs, interests and feelings

		our child
by **listening** carefully to our child's attempts to communicate	→	• feels recognized and special

		our child
by giving him our undivided attention	→	• has the security and encouragement to continue to communicate

Finding time and peace of mind to share precious moments with our children often starts with a very conscious effort, as the following poem relates.

I Took His Hand and Followed

My dishes went unwashed today
I didn't make my bed
I took his hand and followed
Where his eager footsteps led.

Oh yes, we went adventuring
My little child and I
Exploring all the great outdoors
Beneath the sun and sky.

We watched a robin feed her young
We climbed a sunlit hill
Saw cloud-sheep scamper through the sky
We plucked a daffodil.

That my house was so neglected
That I didn't brush the stairs
In twenty years no one on earth
Will know or even care.

But that I've helped my little child
To noble adulthood grow
In twenty years the whole wide world
May look and see and know.

Author unknown

CHAPTER TWO

Adapt to "Share the Moment"

For a child to talk, he must have:
something to say,
the opportunity to say it, and
the encouragement and satisfaction
to make the effort worthwhile.

This chapter is about:

- what we can do to ensure that our children have something to say and have the encouragement they need to make their effort worthwhile.

- ways to let our children know that we are really listening.

- how we can encourage our children to stay in conversations.

- how we can share experiences with our children, even when they don't appear to be able or interested.

Wonderful things start to happen when we take the time to **Observe**, **Wait** for and **Listen** to our children. We find that we begin to understand them better and share some precious moments.

But sometimes OWLing is not enough. There are times when a child doesn't seem interested in connecting with us. Tyler's mom had this problem:

She followed Tyler's lead and talked about what he was doing.

And she tried being the teacher and showed him how to do it.

Then Tyler's mom tried: • Being face to face • Imitating and Interpreting • Taking turns

She **adapted** to share the moment. It worked. She made the connection!

Be Face To Face

One of the most important things we can do to communicate with our child is also one of the simplest: **Position ourselves so that our child can look directly into our eyes.**

"The eyes are the mirror of the soul."

When we are face to face, available and interested, some surprising things happen:

We learn more about our children by being able to observe their facial expressions, focus, state of alertness and skin tone.

Our children learn more about us. They can see the way our mouth moves to form words and watch our eyes to find out what we're looking at. They can also see and experience our acceptance of their attempts to communicate and our pleasure in "sharing the moment" with them.

We talk with our children, not at our children. Being close together encourages the give and take of communication and puts us in a better position to allow the child to lead.

We've all experienced how hard it is to have a conversation with someone taller or shorter than we are. It's such an effort to make eye contact, and we soon move on to talk to someone we are more comfortable with — someone at our level. **So rather than looming over our child, we can:**

- **Bend our knees more**
- **Get down on the floor**
- **Lie on our tummy**
- **Hold our child on our knees**
- **Sit on the floor and give our child the chair**

We can make it easier and more comfortable for our child to look into our eyes and have conversations with us by adapting our position so we are "face to face".

Let Your Child Know You're Listening

Imitate

One of the best ways to connect with very young children who are just beginning to communicate is to imitate their sounds, actions, facial expressions and words. If a child puts his head to one side and we do the same, if he says "uh uh" and we say the same, he will know that we're interested in what he's doing and what he's saying. Chances are we'll make a connection that develops into a conversation.

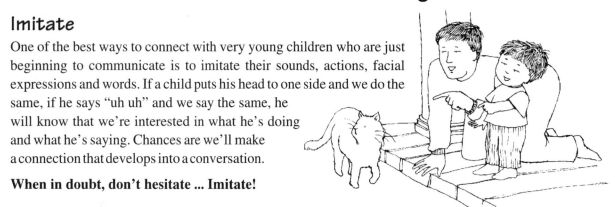

When in doubt, don't hesitate ... Imitate!

Interpret

We get excited about the new sounds and gestures that come from our child. We are quick to interpret them and to assign them the words we think they mean.

When we interpret, it confirms that we've received our child's message. It provides our child with a language model to learn from. We usually think of interpreters in terms of a foreign language, but when we interpret for our child, we're trying to help her speak our language.

When we interpret for our child, we say it as she would if she could.

Interpreting a child who is difficult to understand demands a special kind of detective work.

• Interpreting may mean guessing at what the child's trying to say and putting it into words. Even when we are wrong, our response lets our child know that we are listening.

• Repeating what our child says with a question in our voice encourages her to try again and, perhaps, she can be clearer.

• Explaining that we can't understand and asking our child to show us is another way of confirming our interest.

When all else fails, a sincere expression of our desire to understand and to try again later will let our child know that we appreciate her efforts.

Comment

Commenting on what we are doing when our child appears interested can be the start of sharing information and everyday activities — e.g., setting the table, washing up, sweeping the floor — and perhaps even getting some 'help' in doing them. We also let our child know that we are interested in communicating with her when we comment on what she says or does and **we don't change the topic.**

Have Conversations — Take Turns

When children are learning to communicate, the more conversations they have, the more turns they get to take and the more opportunities they have to learn.

A good conversation, like a good seesaw ride, happens only when each partner takes a turn!

For a child beginning to communicate, **a 'turn' can be a look, a gesture or a sound.** Or a child's turn can even be as subtle as an intake of breath. It may not seem like much, but by recognizing and accepting our child's way of taking part, we can keep the conversation going.

"Conversation" sounds like such a formal adult word. But all it really is, is a series of turns. We take a turn, the child takes a turn, and then we take another turn. As our child matures, her turns in the conversation will progress to words, phrases and sentences.

The natural give and take of daily life with our children gives us many opportunities to share experiences, take turns, exchange ideas, and have good conversations with them. In the beginning, these conversations help our children experience the joy of sharing what's on their minds. Then they discover that these conversations can provide them with new and useful information about their world.

You've "Gotta" Keep the Conversation Going

Sometimes it's hard to keep a conversation going. Often our children don't know what they're supposed to do. It takes time and encouragement for children to learn the art of conversation. In the beginning, they need help.

1. Signal silently

Our facial expressions and actions can show our children that we are waiting for them to take a turn. We can:

- Open our eyes wide with anticipation. Raise an eyebrow or wink to signal that we expect something.

- Smile to encourage our child and show her that we believe she can come through with her turn.

- Silently mouth the word we want our child to say, and then wait.

- Lean toward our child to show her that she has our focus and our interest.

- Point directly to the object or activity to which we want our child to respond.

2. Signal with words

Our voice and our words can also let our children know what we expect of them. We can:

- Say things like "Look" ... "Okay"... "Your turn"... "What's happening now?".

- Repeat what we have said with a questioning intonation or louder.

- Say the same thing in a different way. "Katie want to go for a walk with Mommy?" Then "Katie go outside to see flowers?"

- Change our question to a statement. "Is Tyler hungry?" Then "Tyler wants an apple."

- Change our comment to a question. "It's time to take a bath." Then "Katie want to play in the tub?"

- Shorten the message. "Is Tyler feeling a little hungry?" shortened to "Want a cookie?"

3. Then Wait Wait Wait

Hi and Lois comic strip reprinted with permission — The Toronto Star Syndicate. Copyright: King Features

Our children, like Trixie, need time to collect their thoughts and decide how to respond. When we wait for our children to respond, we let then know that they have something to say.

4. Use good questions

Good questions help a child enter into and stay in conversation. They must be sincere and appropriate to our child's level. Good questions:

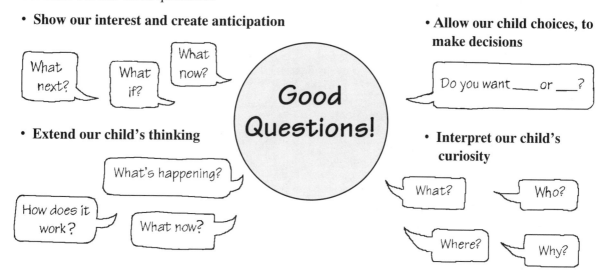

- **Show our interest and create anticipation**

What next? What if? What now?

Good Questions!

- **Allow our child choices, to make decisions**

Do you want ____ or ____ ?

- **Extend our child's thinking**

What's happening? How does it work? What now?

- **Interpret our child's curiosity**

What? Who? Where? Why?

Avoid questions that stop conversations

What's that? What's that? What's that?

Dog. Cat. Car.

CAT DOG CAR

You want milk don't you, Cubby?

Conversation Stoppers: Questions that bombard or demand

Questions that answer themselves

A good question is a powerful conversational hook. It often takes a conscious effort to ask good questions that encourage our child to share his experiences with us. Finding the right question isn't always easy, but our child's response lets us know when we've succeeded.

The type of question to ask and the reason for asking it depend on the child's stage of development.

Levels I & II

Remember Laya and Ben? They don't have any words, but their sounds, facial expressions, and their bodies communicate what they feel. Their parents describe how important questions are in keeping the conversation going:

Laya's Mom often uses a questioning inflection in her voice to find out what Laya's trying to tell her.

> *"When she starts to get restless in her high chair, I shake my head and say 'No more? You're not hungry any more? Want down?' Laya looks when she hears my voice, and I say again 'Want to get down?' Believe me, the questions are genuine, because often I'm not sure what she's trying to tell me."*

Ben's Dad says questions get Ben interested and focused; they hook his attention.

> *"I hear the front door open. I ask, 'Who's there?' , and then I wait. 'Who's coming?' I ask again. I wait and look back and forth between Ben and the door. When he looks, vocalizes, or shows a reaction in any way, I say, 'That's Mommy! Mommy's coming!' The word 'Mommy' has meaning for him. If he hears it often enough, I know, one day soon, he'll understand the word 'Mommy' and may try to say it or sign it."*

Ben's Dad also asks questions to let Ben know that he's waiting for him to take a turn.

> *"Like when Ben and I are face to face, and I'm making funny faces and sounds. I say, 'Funny? Is Daddy being funny?' I wait. Then Ben laughs again, and I ask, 'Daddy do it again?' I wait some more, and Ben wriggles and laughs."*

Level III

Tyler understands quite a few words and simple instructions. He answers his parents by pointing, vocalizing, using eye gaze, or showing them. His non-verbal communication still predominates.

Tyler's Mom describes how her questions help Tyler make decisions:

> *"I ask him questions like 'Tyler, would you like toast or crackers?' 'What do you want to do?' 'What do you need?"*

Tyler's Mom uses questions to encourage Tyler to talk about what's happening:

> *"If I ask things like 'Where's the other car?', 'Who's there?', or 'Where are your shoes?', he tries to tell me."*

> *"I want to give Tyler a chance to express himself as fully as he is able right now. I wait for him to answer, either by showing me or by using the limited number of words in his vocabulary. I try to vary the questions and avoid overusing any one question."*

Level IV

Katie is actually beginning to ask questions like "Where's Mommy?" or "Go up?" She takes turns, and her parents expect verbal answers to their questions. She is also starting to talk about things in the recent past and things which are not visible, which means they can ask her questions about them as well. Here's how they describe the process:

Katie's vocabulary is increasing, but at times she's hard to understand. Katie's mother asks questions when she wants Katie to clarify things she doesn't understand:

When she wants Katie to make choices, for example —

"Which book do you want to read?"
"Where do you want to go?"
"What do you want to eat?"

When she wants Katie to tell her about events, for example —

"Where did you go today?"
"What did you eat for lunch?"
"Who did you see?"

When she wants Katie to explain things, for example —

"What are you doing?"
"What's that for?"
"What's going to happen now?"

"The other day she said, 'gasiga.' I had no idea what she meant, so I repeated 'gasiga?' as a question. Then Katie said 'basiga,' and I knew what she meant. 'Bicycle,' I repeated."

At Level IV, questions to which the answer is "yes" or "no" limit the child's opportunity to respond.

Sharing Isn't Always Easy

Children differ in their interest and ability to communicate. Some children often initiate conversations, but sometimes they don't. Some children usually respond, but sometimes they won't. In the course of an average day, a child may communicate in all of the four communication styles illustrated below.

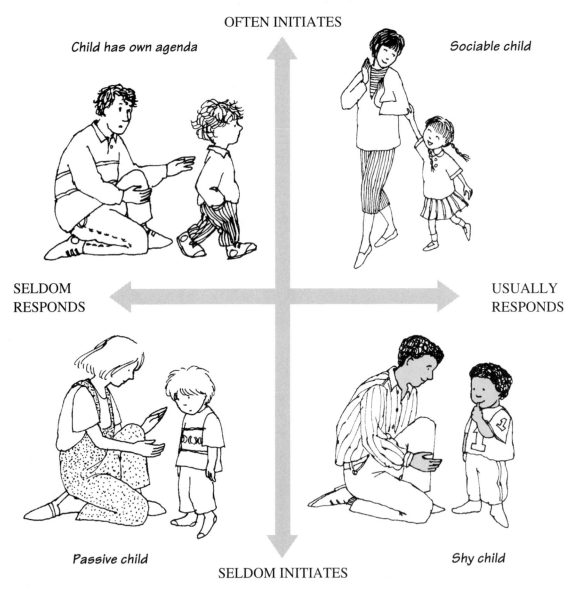

OFTEN INITIATES

Child has own agenda

Sociable child

SELDOM RESPONDS

USUALLY RESPONDS

Passive child

Shy child

SELDOM INITIATES

By being sensitive to our child's repertoire of changing moods and behaviours, we will consciously adapt our own behaviour so that we can share experiences with our child.

Ways to share experiences —
with a child who has his own agenda

*When our child has his own agenda,
he appears not to be interested in ours.*

Taking turns with a child who has his own agenda is indeed a challenge. Only when his attention is focused do we have the opportunity to follow his lead and create a shared experience.

We can create shared experiences when we:

- **Recognize something that our child is particularly interested in doing**

- **Create a high-interest activity** — e.g., ball, water-play, wind-up toys, balloons, bubbles, "peek-a-boo", or music

- **Adapt** the activity or the position of our body **to be face to face** with our child

- **Recognize and accept any of our child's subtle attempts to communicate as being meaningful** — e.g., a quick look, a change in body position, a change in facial expression or voice

- **Have realistic expectations** of the kinds of turns our child can take

- **Imitate** the actions and sounds our child makes

- **Interpret our child's behaviour** to let him know that we accept and respect what he is doing or saying.

Ways to share experiences —
with a child who is passive or shy

When our child is passive, she seldom initiates, appears unable to understand, and shows little interest in connecting with us.

When our child is shy, he usually speaks only when spoken to and doesn't use the communication skills he has.

Instead of taking over for our child and being afraid of those 'silent moments', we can create opportunities for our child to communicate.

We can create opportunities for our child to communicate when we:

- **Tempt our child** with activities that have a special interest for him

- **Repeat pleasurable routines** until our child is able to anticipate what comes next; then wait for our child to respond in his way

- **Adapt** our position **to be face to face** with our child

- **Arouse our child's curiosity** by setting up new high interest opportunities for him to explore

- Take the time to **OWL** (Observe... Wait... and Listen) to our child

- **Gently imitate our child** in play and interpret any subtle attempt to communicate.

Ways to share experiences —
with a child who is sociable

When our child is sociable and enjoys interacting with others but has no words or is difficult to understand, we can help her learn better ways of communicating.

How able and enthusiastic our child will become as a conversational partner depends largely on how we respond to her efforts to communicate.

We can create opportunities for our child to learn when we:

- **Include our child in our daily routines** and take the time to wait for her to participate with us

- Listen carefully and **acknowledge our child's attempts to communicate**

- **Interpret our child's message.** Say it as she would if she could say it correctly

- **Continue the conversation** by making statements and comments on our child's topic

- **Save questions for times when we genuinely want to know what our child is thinking.**

The pleasure our child feels and the success she experiences when the two of us 'talk' together will give her the self-confidence to try again.

Conversations — How They Grow and Change

We have conversations with our children long before they can talk in words. The kind of conversations we can expect to have will depend on our child's stage of development.

Conversations with a child at Level I

We can "share the moment" with our child whenever we notice her reaction to something and follow her interests.

> *Mom noticed Laya looking up at the mobile overhead and commented, "Bears, you're looking at the bears."*
>
> *Laya kept looking.*
>
> *Mom interpreted Laya's look and said what Laya would say if she could, "The bears are dancing."*

They shared the moment. They were having a conversation.

We can also share experiences with our child when she responds to us.

> *Laya was lying in her crib, but not asleep.*
>
> *Mom came to the side of the crib and shook Laya's rattle and waited.*
>
> *Laya moved her body slightly.*
>
> *Mom shook the rattle again and waited.*
>
> *Laya turned towards the sound.*
>
> *Mom shook the rattle again and waited.*
>
> *Laya looked at her mom.*
>
> *Mom smiled, shook the rattle once more, and waited.*
>
> *Laya looked away.*
>
> *Mom interpreted Laya's message and said what Laya would say if she could, "Enough of the rattle for now."*

In the beginning, it is our sensitivity to our child's behaviour that creates the shared moments which are so critical to our child's feelings of security and self-confidence.

Conversations with a child at Level II

At this level, our children show their interest more clearly. They deliberately look, reach, and vocalize, and they actively explore objects by reaching, mouthing, shaking, and banging.

Conversations can happen when we respond to our child.

Ben and his father were playing with a teddy bear on the sofa.

Dad accidentally knocked the bear onto the floor.

Ben looked at the bear.

Dad interpreted Ben's look and said what Ben would say if he could, "Teddy fell down," and then Dad waited.

Ben reached for the bear, chewed on it, looked at his father and laughed.

Dad commented, "Ben, you love your teddy."

> *Conversations can happen spontaneously when we observe our child's reactions and let him know that we are interested.*

Conversations can also happen when our child responds to us.

He's really paying attention to me. That's part of the conversation.

Dad was blowing up balloons for Ben and then letting the air out to make the balloons fly away.

Ben watched with wonder.

Dad blew up another balloon and held onto it and waited.

Ben reached out to touch the balloon. Dad placed the balloon closer to Ben and said what he thought Ben would say if he could, "Balloon, want the balloon," and waited.

Ben put both hands on the balloon. Dad let go, and the balloon quickly deflated.

Ben handed the balloon back to Dad. Dad took the balloon and said what he thought Ben would say, "Blow, blow balloon," and waited.

Ben pushed the balloon toward Dad's mouth. Dad nodded and said, "Okay. Daddy'll blow."

And Daddy blew up that balloon many times.

> *Conversations happen spontaneously when we create interesting activities or routines with our child and wait for his response.*

Conversations with a child at Level III

At Level III, our children reach an exciting milestone in language development. They begin to talk about the world in single words or signs, and they want to share their understanding with us.

Our child is encouraged to join us in conversation when we respond to him.

Tyler ran up to a big oak tree and poked it, saying "Tee-tee", and then looked at his sister.

Lisa bent down beside him, nodded and interpreted by saying what Tyler would say if he could, "A tree," and then she waited.

Tyler repeated "Tee", nodded and smiled at Lisa.

Lisa nodded back to Tyler and commented, "A big tree."

Good conversations often happen when we go exploring

Conversations can also begin when our child responds to us.

Tyler's Dad was getting ready to go outside for a walk and noticed Tyler sitting on the floor with a toy. He asked, "Tyler, do you want to go outside?"

Tyler looked up at his Dad.

Dad shortened his question: "Want to go out?"

Tyler got up, walked over to his Dad at the door and said, "Ow."

Dad smiled and said, "Out, okay. We'll go outside together."

This level is a good time to include our children in our daily routines, like washing dishes, sorting laundry, or shopping for groceries. Participating in these activities gives our children a broader understanding of our world as well as theirs.

And this understanding will open the door to new experiences, new language and new conversations.

At this point in a child's development, he talks best about what he can see, hear and touch, so most conversations are still about the present moment.

Conversations with a child at Level IV

At this level, the possibilities for conversations multiply. Our children are using a large number of single words and/or signs, some memorized short phrases, and perhaps a few creative combinations of words. Our children start to describe things in more detail.

Conversations happen when we respond to our child.

> *Katie was in her pajamas. She pointed down to her bare feet and said, "Soo."*
>
> *Mom was puzzled and asked, "Shoe?"*
>
> *Katie looked up and said, "Daddy."*
>
> *Mom remembered that Katie had been to the shoe repair shop with her Dad and interpreted by saying what Katie would say if she could. "Daddy's shoes. You went to get Daddy's shoes."*
>
> *Katie smiled and said, "Bye-bye Grampa."*
>
> *Mom thought for a moment, realized what Katie meant, and again interpreted: "You said bye-bye to the old man in the shoe shop."*
>
> *Katie smiled and nodded.*

Katie and her mother had their first conversation about an event in Katie's memory.

At this point, conversations can get more complex. They happen when our child responds to us.

> *Mom was helping Katie get dressed. She held up Katie's sock and said, "Sock."*
>
> *Katie picked up the sock, showed it to her Mom and said, "Katie's sock."*

"I'll never forget when this happened," said Katie's Mom. "Katie added on to something I said. It was great."

Knowing what our child is feeling and thinking isn't always easy. We can make the connections that help our child communicate and learn by taking the time to OWL,   • *allowing our child to lead, and*

            • *adapting our behaviour to share the moment.*

In summary,

when we **adapt** to share the moment:

---

by **being face to face** with our child

our child
- senses our interest in what he is doing or saying
- is more likely to include us in his play
- becomes more aware of what we do and say

---

by **imitating** our child's actions, sounds, or words

our child
- knows that what he did or said was noticed and valued
- may repeat what he did a second time so that a fun taking-turns game may follow

---

by **interpreting** our child's attempts to communicate

our child
- feels that he has been heard
- knows that we are trying to understand him
- sees the correct action or hears the correct word for what he is attempting to do or say

---

by **waiting** with anticipation for our child to take a turn

our child
- feels that his participation is expected and valued
- recognizes when to take his turn
- is more likely to try to communicate and take an active part

---

by **commenting** on what's happening or asking questions that are genuine and geared to our child's level

our child
- is aware that we are interested in him and what he has to say
- may try to respond

---

by **being sensitive** to our child's repertoire of changing moods and behaviours

our child
- is aware that we are interested in him and what he has to say
- may try to respond

CHAPTER THREE

Add Language and Experience

"The most significant act of learning of our early life, perhaps of our whole life, is the acquisition of our mother tongue. Once we have language at our disposal, we have a key which will unlock many doors."

David Crystal, linguist

This chapter is about:

- what we can say and do to help our child understand and learn language.

- ways of highlighting information so that it's easier for our child to absorb it.

- adding language and experience appropriate to our child's level of development.

- making the moments we share with our children richer in opportunities for them to improve their ability to communicate.

Learning Language Begins at Birth

When our child behaves in ways that are easy to understand, we instinctively adapt to share these moments and we add information. Without thinking about it, we make many adjustments to our way of talking that help our child learn. It happens so easily and naturally when our child is healthy and we're relaxed and responsive.

We **Match** our child's actions, sounds or words to confirm that we have heard him.

We **Model** the correct language to provide our child with the information he needs to express himself.

We **Add More** information to help our child understand more about what's happening.

Sometimes, however, making the connections that help our child learn is not easy, and we're frustrated when our child's behaviours are hard to understand. We don't know what our child needs or how to help him understand what we mean.

*It really **does take two to talk**, and when our child does not play his part by giving us the clues we expect and need, we become anxious and confused about how to play our part.*

*This chapter confirms and reminds us of what we, as parents, already instinctively know — ways to **reach** our child so that we can **teach** our child.*

Learning language takes time

We all hope that our child will learn to use language effectively, and it is frustrating at times when progress is slow. At first, our child needs time just to take in information and to improve his ability to understand what is being said, what words really mean. Even when our child is not yet talking, he is learning a lot about connecting and communicating.

And when our child starts to communicate and directs clear messages to us, it's important to be realistic about what we can expect. If our child is pointing and making sounds, we can't expect him to say "milk" right away. Maybe the next step will just be "mmmmm". Hearing us repeat "milk" many times is what he needs to help him say the word better.

The extra information we add will help our child progress:
- from hearing words to understanding them
- from a random movement to a recognizable gesture
- from not imitating to being able to imitate
- from gestures to using sounds to communicate
- from imprecise sounds to ones that are closer to the real word
- from words to phrases and sentences
- from incorrect grammar to the correct form

When our child doesn't attempt to use the information that we add, it may be that he is not yet able to. We need to continue to provide him with opportunities to learn — our careful observation makes us more aware of our child's communication level, so we won't make the mistake of giving information that is too difficult for him to learn.

Achieving the goal of distinct words, signs, or picture-pointing takes time. We will have to emphasize and repeat on many different occasions before the new information becomes well established as part of our child's repertoire. Only then can we begin to expect more.

When To Add Language and Experience

1. In the give and take of daily routines — we can add information

We share a lot of moments with our children during the ordinary routines of daily living.

When we're with our children and we describe what is happening, we give them the words they need to understand and, later, to use language. Daily activities provide a prime time for learning because our children can hear the same words repeated over and over again in these familiar situations:

- going up and down stairs
- waking up
- getting the diaper changed
- going to the bathroom
- brushing teeth
- combing hair
- getting dressed
- mealtime and snack time
- putting on hats and coats to go out
- picking up toys
- having a bath
- getting ready for bed

Although our household chores may take longer to do when we involve our children, these experiences enrich their opportunities to understand and learn. Our children love being with us, and they can learn so much when:

- setting the table
- preparing a meal
- baking a cake, pie, muffins
- unloading the dryer
- buying groceries
- putting away groceries
- opening mail
- shovelling snow
- raking leaves
- washing the car
- washing dishes
- making beds
- getting into the car (seatbelts, car seat)
- locking and unlocking the door
- turning lights on and off

First comes experience, then understanding, and finally language

We help our children understand their experiences when we talk about what's happening or what's going to happen. We stimulate them to use language when we consistently repeat the same words over and over again in familiar situations.

Tyler's mother describes how Tyler gradually learned how to use the word "BATH".

First comes the *Experience*

"At first, Tyler heard the sound of running water and looked to see where it was coming from. I said, 'It's your BATH. I'm pouring water for your BATH.' Tyler didn't understand the words, but he felt the warmth of the water, heard the sound of the splashing, and began to experience bathtime."

Then comes *Understanding*

"This went on for several months, and then I noticed that Tyler began to kick and wriggle when I was undressing him. I'd say, 'Time for Tyler's BATH. Are you ready for a BATH?' And he would wriggle more. He had started to understand what was going to happen.

"Finally, one night after dinner, Tyler was playing with his blocks, and I said, 'It's your BATH. Come, let's get ready for a BATH.' He dropped the blocks and reached up to be carried to the bathroom. He really understood what I was saying."

And then comes *Language*

"Time went on, and Tyler began to make sounds like real words. One night I decided to ask him, 'You know what time it is, Tyler? It's your...' And I waited. He replied 'Ba.' I repeated, 'BATH. Yes, it's your BATH. You said it, Tyler, BATH.' We had started to communicate with words."

2. When our child shows interest — we can add information

Giving a child what she wants, but holding on to it tightly for a few seconds, gives us the chance to "share the moment" and add the words that will help her learn.

At first, when we recognize what our children are interested in, we are so happy we understand them that we often give them what they want right away. But we can use these opportunities to let them hear, see, or feel the specific information that will help them understand and eventually use language.

When a child shows interest, take advantage of the moment. Our children are more eager to listen and try something new when we talk about what really interests them.

3. When something unusual happens — we can add information

uh-oh!

When a spoon drops, a button pops, there's a loud knock or a missing sock ... it surprises us and gets our attention. The interest it creates makes it easy to "share the moment" and is a good time to add the information that will help our child to learn.

4. When things go wrong — we can explain and add information

When our child writes on the wall, won't share his ball, spills the juice, lets the dog loose, we can use these opportunities to explain what's wrong, why it happened and what would be better.

Oh my! Walls are not for writing on. Paper is!

When something unusual happens, or when things go wrong, a child will learn if we explain:
- what happened
- why it happened
- how to make the experience "okay"

How to Add Language and Experience

Hi and Lois comic strip reprinted with permission — The Toronto Star Syndicate. Copyright: King Features

Trixie is right. What good is saying "swing" if you can't say "push"? We can help our children learn the new words they need when we imitate what they say and add one word.

1. Imitate and add

One of the easiest ways to help our child learn to communicate is to imitate his sounds and/or gestures, and then add a new word or action. If we expect our child to imitate *us*, we have to use words that are possible for him to say.

When we add a new word or action to what our child already knows, the new information we add is more likely to be understood.

It's a simple process:
- *say what the child says*
- *do what the child does*
- *then add another word or action connected to the one we've just imitated.*

2. Interpret

Interpreting what our child is feeling or wanting by using the words and/or actions that she would use if she could communicate more clearly is a sensitive and effective way of letting our child know that we understand her. It also gives her the information she needs at the very moment she needs it.

If we consistently give our children a model they can follow, in time the words will become familiar to them, and then — oh joy! On that greatest of all days, they will actually begin to use these words.

Saying what our child would say if she could say it lets our child know we understand her, and gives her a language model that will help her learn.

3. Expand

In the early stages of our child's development, it's important to keep our language simple. But it's easy to get stuck in a pattern of using only one- and two-word phrases or of responding with the same "pat" words. This limited style can soon feel stilted and unnatural, and it also limits our child's opportunities to learn.

When we expand on the messages that our child gives us:

• It helps our child understand more about what he experiences.
• It helps our child learn to say new words.

Depending on the child's level of understanding, we can expand on any topic in many ways.

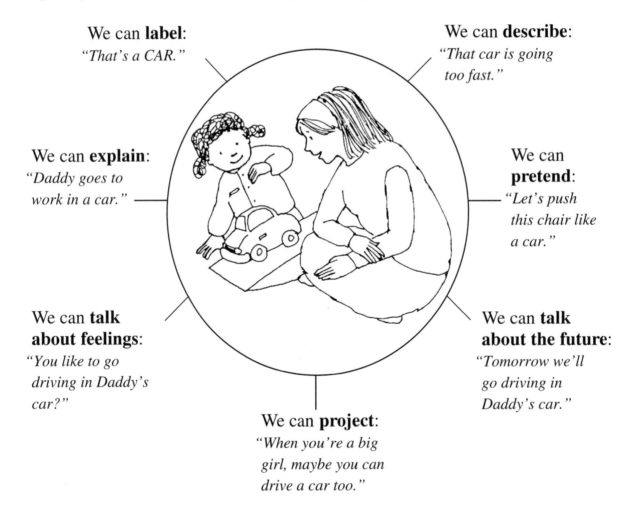

We can **label**:
"That's a CAR."

We can **describe**:
"That car is going too fast."

We can **explain**:
"Daddy goes to work in a car."

We can **pretend**:
"Let's push this chair like a car."

We can **talk about feelings**:
"You like to go driving in Daddy's car?"

We can **talk about the future**:
"Tomorrow we'll go driving in Daddy's car."

We can **project**:
"When you're a big girl, maybe you can drive a car too."

Take a moment to draw or write on the picture an activity that your child enjoys. Along the sides, write in the words you could add to help your child learn more about the activity.

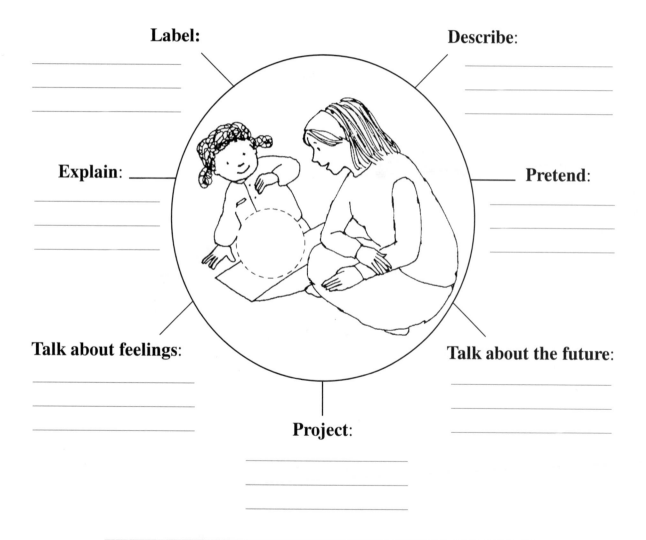

Label: _____

Describe: _____

Explain: _____

Pretend: _____

Talk about feelings: _____

Talk about the future: _____

Project: _____

Expanding on the child's message gives him the chance to hear new words and gradually to understand them.

Ways of Highlighting Information

1. Gesture

Gestures are wonderful! They come so naturally to us: a shiver, a smile, a shrug. Gestures are an effective and often overlooked way of helping our child understand language. Gestures capture our child's interest and focus her attention.

They give information — like when we shake our heads from side to side and say, "No more".

They show emotion — like when our arms open wide to welcome our child's warm little body.

They convey attitude — like when a smile and nodding head indicate how much our child wants to share that ice cream cone.

Our children love it when we use big gestures. It stimulates their imagination and creativity, which are both important for language learning.

Gestures also give our child a way of expressing herself before she is able to talk. Arms up to say "Lift me up"; a wave to say "Bye-bye"; a head shake to say "No" or "Yes"; a hug to say "I love you"; and many, many more...

Using a gesture is like painting a picture to go along with the words we are saying. In the beginning, it's the simple gestures we make that help our child learn.

We help our child put a word to the action when we:
- *are consistent*
- *are face to face with our child*
- *say the word and make the gesture at the same time*

2. Emphasize key words

Laya's father talked in short, simple phrases and had fun exaggerating words and sounds to help Laya learn the word 'JELLO'.

DAD: *(Points to dessert.)* Look, Laya, ... JELLO.

LAYA: (Looks.)

DAD: It's your favorite JELLO.

LAYA: (Looks. Eyes widen. Leans forward slightly.)

DAD: It's STRAWBERRY JELLOOOO! *(He gives Laya a spoonful.)*

LAYA: (Swallows Jello. Looks at Dad.)

DAD: MMMMMMMMMM! That was good JELLO!

Like Laya's Dad, we can help our children learn when we

- **Pause before the key word** ("Do you want... Jello?")

- **Prolong the key word** ("Jellooooo.")

- **Whisper or shout the key word**

- **Point at the object connected with the key word**

Did you ever think a bowl of Jello could open up new doors to communication?

> *Emphasizing adds special interest and fun to words, and it highlights information the child needs to start learning.*

3. Repeat

As adults, we usually understand a word after hearing it once or twice in context. That's not the case with children. Some children need ten repetitions of a word before they attempt it, while others need a hundred repetitions! There are no "rules", no "right number" of repetitions. Our children's actions, gestures, or words tell us when they have absorbed what we have to say. **It's a good idea to find as many different ways as possible of using the same word**. For example, when undressing our child, we can find different ways to use the word "off":

Consistently repeating the same words every time we carry out a routine will help our child understand and later be able to use those words.

In the beginning, our child may not be able to understand or say the words we use. But the more often she hears words associated with particular objects, the easier it will be for her to understand what we are saying ... and, finally, to use those words. **Repetition is crucial!**

Repetition helps a child learn

The Family Circle comic strip reprinted with permission — The Toronto Star Syndicate. Copyright: King Features

Copyright 1978, The Register and Tribune Syndicate, Inc.

Add Language and Experience Appropriate to the Child's Development

The first words that most children experience and understand are deeply rooted in who and what they see every day — Mommy, Daddy, spoon, dish, bottle, bed, blanket, bear. But before our child can use these words, there are a number of levels through which we have to guide him.

Too much, too soon can intimidate a child, but too little, too late can frustrate a child. *It's important for us to know what to do at Levels 1 and II, where to be at Level III, and not to ignore Level IV.*

When our child is at **Level I**, we interpret his sounds and body language. His smiles, cries, screams, and wriggles succeed in communicating to us his feelings and needs.

At **Level II**, although our child is still not communicating in a conventional way, we can interpret his facial expressions, body language and sounds as he begins to reach out and explore his environment. At these two early levels, we play a critical role in helping our child become aware of the power and pleasure of communication.

What to do at Levels I & II:

- **Imitate** our child's sounds and actions; then add something new

- **Use gestures**

- **Interpret** — say it as he would, if he could

- **Show the objects** you are talking about to the child

- **Name people and label things** in which he shows interest

- **Talk in simple sentences** about what's happening

- **Emphasize key words**

- **Repeat and be consistent**

Level I Instead of...   ...Add information

Level II Instead of...   ...Add information

At **Level III**, our child develops that all-important interest in connecting with those around him. He looks to make sure we are paying attention to what interests him. Speech is emerging, and he may point, gesture, act out or makes sounds that stand for a word.

Where to be at Level III:

- **Imitate and add**

- **Interpret**

- **Emphasize words** our child may be able to imitate and express

- **Expand** — add slightly longer phrases he can understand, even if he can't say them.

- **Vary what you talk about** — discuss different people, events, objects, locations, actions, feelings, descriptive qualities, etc.

- **Repeat and be consistent**

| Level III | Instead of... | ...Add information |

As our child moves into **Level IV**, he will begin to use words, signs, and phrases consistently, even though they may be hard to understand. And we can continue to help our child understand and say more.

Don't ignore Level IV:

- **Emphasize key words** which our child can imitate in short sentences

- **Keep expanding** — add longer comments on the topic

- **Link our child's comment to a past experience**

- **Talk about what will happen next**

- **Pretend and imagine** what might happen "if "...

| Level IV | Instead of... | ...Add information |

Adding Information is easier than it seems

At Level I

Laya and her mother were able to turn the discomfort of a cold into an experience they both could learn from and enjoy.

LAYA: (Has a runny nose; sniffles.)

MOM: Oh, your NOSE is runny. *Interprets. Emphasizes key word.* I'm going to get a tissue for your NOSE. *Talks about what's going to happen. Repeats.*

LAYA: (Watches her mother.)

MOM: I'm going to wipe your NOSE. *Repeats.* (Turns the nose wiping into a game.) Now, I wipe my NOSE. *Gestures and emphasizes key word.*

LAYA: (Wriggles and laughs.)

MOM: You liked that! *Interprets.* I'm going to wipe teddy's NOSE. *Repeats.*

At Level II

Ben's mother was able to add information and experience while they were sitting outside on a beautiful summer afternoon.

BEN: (Sitting outside with his Mom when a plane roars overhead. He stops moving and stares.)

MOM: Oh, PLANE! *Interprets.* You heard the PLANE! *Repeats.* There's a big PLANE up in the sky! *Emphasizes key words. Repeats. Expands.*

BEN: (Is startled when the screen door slams.)

MOM: Uh, oh... did that scare you? *Expresses feelings.* Grandpa opened the door. *Talks about what is happening.*

At Level III

Do you remember Tyler and his Mom? Well, they're finding new ways to add information and experience at every playtime.

TYLER: (Sits on the floor, turning the pages of a newspaper.)

MOM: (Gets down on floor and puts paper over his head.) Peek-a-boo! *Expands on the game.*

TYLER: (Pulls paper off and climbs onto kitchen chair.) Chair.

MOM: Yes... Daddy's chair. *Expands and emphasizes key words.* Daddy's not here today. Daddy's at work. *Explains.*

TYLER: Uk.

MOM: Work... yes, Daddy's at work. *Interprets.*

At Level IV

Here's a small example of how Katie's Grandma adds information and experience when Katie comes to visit.

KATIE: (Arrives at Grandma's house and points to where the Christmas tree had been.) Tree... tree!

GRANDMA: Yes, Christmas tree! *Expands.* That's where Grandma had the Christmas tree. *Links to past experience.*

KATIE: (While being tucked into bed.) Muffin store...

GRANDMA: Muffin store. *Repeats.* You like the muffin store, don't you? *Interprets.* We'll go there tomorrow. *Talks about the future.*

In summary,

when we **a**dd language and actions:

oh. oh.

Oh a **hole**. A big **hole** in your pants.

by **using facial expressions and gestures** when we talk	→	**our child** • finds it easier to understand our words • learns a way of expressing himself before he is able to talk
by **imitating** what our child does or says **and adding a word or action** connected to it	→	**our child** • is exposed to information at a time when he is interested
by **interpreting** our child's feelings or wants	→	**our child** • has the opportunity to hear the words he wants to say when he needs them
by **exaggerating sounds or key words**	→	**our child** • finds it easier to focus on the new sounds or words and to associate them with what is happening
by **repeating** the same words or phrases every time we play a game	→	**our child** • finds it easier to understand and then say the word • begins to anticipate what comes next
by **expanding** on what our child is doing or saying	→	**our child** • is exposed to a wealth of new ideas and language connected to what he is interested in • comes to understand how objects and events are associated • learns language to express more complete ideas

Treat Yourself

Until we get used to it, constantly thinking about what we say to our child can be draining. Sure, our child's progress is rewarding to us. That's what gives us the strength to carry on, but we'll all benefit from a little extra encouragement. Dinner at a favorite restaurant perhaps? Having someone else cook supper? When our child has learned a new skill, let's treat ourselves to something special. We deserve it.

CHAPTER FOUR

Play the 3a Way

"Ah, to see the world through the eyes of a child, where there is wonder in all things and where boredom or routine do not exist."

Linda and Richard Eyre, parents and authors

This chapter is about:

- the power of play and how it can provide us with opportunities to help our children learn to connect with us.

- our special role in making play both pleasurable and purposeful.

- how we can make it easier for our children to learn specific steps toward communication WHILE PLAYING by:

    — dreaming of communication goals for our children that are realistic

    — planning appropriate play activities

    — sharing play the 3a way.

The Power of Play

Play is social and fun

Our children play for the sake of playing — because they enjoy it. They are not consciously trying to improve their motor skills, practise new sounds, or make connections with others — yet these are important benefits that happen through play. When our children are having a good time playing with us, they learn in a natural way.

Play encourages taking turns

If our children are going to learn to communicate, they must get involved in two-way interactions. Taking turns with actions or words is the essential element of shared play and of conversation. "I take a turn; then you take a turn", and so on!

Play is easy to respond to, even without words

One of the benefits of play is that children will respond to it, even if they have a limited ability or desire to talk. The active side of play — like falling down in "Ring around the Rosie", or clapping in "If You're Happy and You Know It"— gives children who have trouble talking a chance to take part. In addition, play helps children connect physical actions with the words that describe those actions — the best way to reinforce understanding and learning.

Play involves repetition

It's possible to repeat words and actions more often in a play activity than it is during our daily activities. We can't pour David's milk ten times at breakfast, but we can spend hours pouring water in the bathtub, having a pretend tea party, or singing "This is the way we pour our milk."

Play integrates many of the senses

Our children are more likely to learn and remember what we're talking about when they see, hear, feel, smell and taste it. If they hear the word "apple" — and see it, feel its roundness, smell it and taste it — they are more likely to understand "apple" and be able to use the word later. Learning is strengthened when several senses send the same message to the brain.

Play is one of the best ways for our children to learn how to communicate and to get along with others.

Our Roles in Play

To get our child's attention, we play **THE ENTERTAINER,** jumping up and down, doing anything to keep our child amused. But sometimes we forget to give our child a chance to join in.

To teach our child, we play **THE DIRECTOR,** demonstrating and instructing, but all too often when we want to teach, we totally dominate the interaction.

When we're not quite sure how to join in, we sit back and play **THE OBSERVER,** watching or providing a play-by-play commentary about what our child is doing. It's a good place to start, but it's definitely not enough.

When we take on the role of **THE RESPONSIVE PARTNER** and take the time to:

adapt to encourage our child to take her turn

add information to help our child learn

allow our child to lead

we make it easier for our child to play and learn.

The Power of Play —
Helping Our Child Learn to Communicate

I wish my child could talk.

I'm going to help him learn to say "Ma for Mom"!

"In the process of achieving anything worthwhile there are three stages: the dreaming, the planning and the doing."

Will Manolson, parent and farmer

In the process of helping our children learn to communicate, play offers us fantastic opportunities to:

- **DREAM** of a specific and realistic communication goal that our child can attain

- **PLAN** for a play activity which has within it opportunities for our child to learn

- **DO** — by sharing the play experiences with our child in ways that make it easier for him to learn

The steps a child usually takes in learning to communicate are outlined at the end of this chapter. This list may help you choose a communication goal for your child.

The Dream — Of a goal which is realistic for our child

We all know that dreams are attained not through wish fairies but through what WE do to help our children take those small steps to reach their potential.

The steps we choose for our child should be:

REALISTIC: A step is attainable only if it originates from our child's present ability to communicate. Long-term dreams like "I wish my child could talk" can be broken down into small steps, beginning with something as simple as reaching for a book.

Questions that can help us choose a realistic step for our child are:
• What gesture, sound, word, or sentence would help our child communicate better?
• What is our child trying to communicate but is unable to?

SPECIFIC: The more specific we are in our own minds about what is realistic for our child to attempt, the clearer we can be about how we can adapt our behaviour to encourage her progress. We can aim for a step as specific as imitating, taking a turn, a gesture for "no more", or a sound like "uh" for "up", or asking ourselves:

• What activity does our child enjoy?
• What communication skills come naturally from that activity?
• What is our child trying to communicate?

USEFUL: Words or gestures that our child can use and repeat often — words like "cup" or "sock" — are better than "tiger"... unless, of course, you happen to have a pet tiger! Choosing words that are useful in everyday life will give our child the opportunity to learn the gestures or words that will help her ask for what she needs or wants.

FUN: We can try the "Lonely Island Game". First we imagine we are on a far-away island, alone with our child. Then we think of how our child communicates with us now, and we ask ourselves: "What could our child learn as a next step that would make our time together on this island more enjoyable?" (The goal can be anything from a nod, to a sound, to speaking in sentences.)

Let's be realistic... and not worry about choosing the perfect goal! If it's too easy or too hard, we'll find out soon enough and be able to adjust accordingly.

The Plan — For an activity that our child will enjoy

Capitalize on strengths

We know what our child enjoys and is especially good at. Perhaps it's moving to music, or looking at books, or crumpling paper. Let's create play activities that take advantage of what our child likes and can do.

Include old favorites

We don't have to plan a new activity every day. A child who enjoys new stories still loves to hear old favorites. Don't leave his old skills and interests behind; often he will want to go back to tried and true activities. Our child benefits from lots and lots of repetition, so we'll use the same song, book, game or art activity many times. The sense of security a child gains from something familiar gives him the confidence to try something new.

Try something new

We should try to explore games, books or crafts that our child has never attempted; generally we should choose a project that he is able to do easily and succeed at. But sometimes it's a good idea to try something just above his skill level. We may have underestimated his talents. Who knows, it may be more fun than we think!

Ideas for play activities and the developmental charts in the following chapters will help us choose activities that are appropriate for our child.

Have fun — go with the flow!

Forced play has no purpose. We shouldn't pressure our child to continue an activity that isn't pleasurable for him. If it's not fun, let's allow our child to lead, to change the direction. Often the best things happen when we are spontaneous and just go with the flow.

Make alternative plans

The best-made plans sometimes go awry. It's a good idea to have alternatives in mind. For example, if we've decided to build with blocks and our child shows no interest, we can toss the blocks into a box, or hide the blocks for our child to find, or turn the blocks into a long train for our child to push. Very often, quick thinking and a change of plan will turn a frustrating moment into a fun time!

Th Doing — By playing the 3a way

Now that we have a realistic dream of what we want our child to learn while playing, and we have planned an activity that will support that learning, the next step is to MAKE IT HAPPEN.

To make it happen, we start by ADAPTING the activity and/or our behaviour to share the play, ADDING language to help our child learn, and always being willing to ALLOW our child to lead.

We adapt to "share the moment" and share the activity by:

- being face to face
- letting our child know we're listening
  - imitating
  - interpreting
  - commenting
  - asking questions
  - taking turns

We add information and experience by:

- imitating and adding
- interpreting
- expanding
  - describing
  - explaining
  - talking about feelings
  - pretending
  - talking about the future

We allow our child to lead by:

- Observing — so we can get to know and understand our child better
- Waiting — to give our child the time he needs to express his interests and feelings
- Listening — so we can respond more sensitively to our child

Ideas for Communication Goals

At First – Imitation

1. Motor imitation without toys

- puff your cheeks full of air
- touch your shoe, toe
- jump up and down
- point your finger
- shake your head
- touch your head
- lick your lips
- clap your hands
- open your mouth
- stick out your tongue
- put palms up in a "gimme five" sign

PAT-A-CAKE

- put your hand on your mouth (yawn)
- raise your arms above your head
- bite on your bottom lip
- make "kissing" movements with lips and hands
- stand up
- wave bye
- make a fist
- touch the floor
- cover your eyes with your hands (Peek-a-boo)

2. Motor imitation using toys and household objects

- pat or feed the doll; put the doll to sleep
- dump the blocks out of the truck
- put a hat on a doll or self
- squeeze a squeaky toy
- hit a xylophone
- put a block in a cup
- push the car
- roll, throw the ball
- turn the pages of a book
- ring a bell
- knock the blocks over
- swing the keys; unlock the door
- put the blocks in the truck
- fly a plane
- stir with a spoon
- put a small can in a large can
- build with two or three blocks
- draw with crayons, paints, markers, pudding

- open and close a lunch box, a drawer, purse
- pretend to sleep on the pillow
- turn the light on and off
- put on a shoe, sunglasses
- push or get in a wagon
- wind a musical toy
- climb in and out of a box
- comb hair
- wash face
- brush teeth
- drink
- go under the table
- crush or tear paper
- eat
- pull a pull toy
- wipe nose
- hit a drum
- stack, empty and fill cartons, containers

3. Transition from motor to sound imitation

It is often helpful to associate an action with a sound in order to focus the child's attention on imitating sounds:

- "Peek" — uncovering eyes
- "M-m-m" (good) — rubbing stomach
- "So-o-o" (big) — raise arms
- "Oops!" — toy falling
- "Razzing" sound — tongue vibrating between lips
- "Bye-Bye"— wave
- "Pat" (a cake) — clap
- "Mm" — car motor sound; pushing car
- Indian war whoop ("wah-wah") — hand over mouth

If your child doesn't imitate speech sounds, start with non-speech sounds:

- blowing — bubbles, a candle or feather
- smacking lips — kiss and make a smacking sound
- cry sound — imitate the little breathy sounds
- sneezing — exaggerate the look and or coughing sound
- animal sounds —

dog: bow-wow or ruff	cow: moo-ooo
cat: meow	sheep: baa-aa
bee: buzz-zz	horse: neigh
goose: honk	chick: peep

4. Then — early single words

apple

Food	Body Parts	Household Objects	Clothing	Outside Objects	Toys	Important People
apple	head	tub/bath	sock	tree	bus	Daddy
bread	hand	bed	shirt	flower	truck	Mommy
meat	legs	TV	pants	grass	horse	names of pets
milk	eyes	sofa	dress	moon	bell	names of friends
juice	hair	sink	coat	sun	train	names of siblings
soup	nose	table	shoe	snow	boat	boy
banana	foot	chair	hat	rain	book	girl
cake	toes	room	bib	dog	ball	baby
pudding		light		cat	blocks	child's name
water		wall		plane		teacher
drink		floor		car		Grandma
cookie		brush		bike		Grandpa
candy		comb		school		
ice cream		pen		bus		
pop		paper				
		cup				
		dish				
		keys				
		soap				
		spoon				
		glasses				
		watch				
		clock				
		pillow				
		money				

Words that Describe

hot	all gone
more	dirty
my	clean
big	broke
wet	nice
cold	on, off
pretty	all done

Social Words

oh-oh	no
hi, hello	enough, nuff
bye	yes
okay	hey
sorry	fine (answer
nite-nite	to "How
	are you?")

Words that Express Feelings

sad	kiss/hug	mad
happy	angry	darn or shoot

Early Action and Action Related Words

play	run	roll
brush	walk	hug
bounce	sleep	gimme
shake	go	hide
blow	push	bang
dance	throw	read
paint	roll	help
feel	sit	pick up
cry	jump	break
hear	drink	pour
pull	clap	fall
wipe	stand	hurt
march	dump	eat
open	look	tickle
kick	close	see
hit	wash	find
stop it	write	blow
catch	hold	rock
sit	tickle	get
giddiup	swing	drop
again	sing	fly
lie down	count	turn around
come	keep	feed
peek	shake	touch
ride	buy	kiss
look	give	come

Location Words

here	out
down	there
in	up
on	under

5. Later — two word phrases

Here are some examples of common combinations:

> throw
> ball

Action + Object

throw ball	eat apple	brush teeth
push car	wipe table	kiss baby
wash hands	shake hand(s)	wash dish
wash face	blow bubble	see Scott (in
open door	pat bunny	mirror)
touch foot	pour milk	play music
read book	clap hands	squirt water
drink juice	hit drum	help me
ride horse	go potty	watch me

Noun + Action

car go	you stand	Dad walk	you paint
horse jump	I write	Mom dance	Mom wash
doll sleep	horse rock	boy ride	chair rock
block fall	girl march	cars crash	

Noun/Action + Location

sit down	on table	fall down	slide down
jump up	walk here	book there	come here
in box	go out	on floor	in bed

Descriptive Words + Noun/Action

big ball	cowboy hat
more cookies, more juice	light's on
wet soap	no bed (won't go to bed)
hot tea, hot stove	TV's on
my car, my dog	dirty face
all gone — soup	Mommy's book

Social Language

You're welcome	Thank you
How are you?	Fine
Please	

6. Still Later — three and four word phrases

> Mom read book

Carrier Phrases

I want   I see   I like

Agent + Action + Object

I throw ball	Steve pet dog	I cut paper
Dad push car	Diane wear shirt	Eric ride horse
Mom read book	I hear music	Karen paint picture
you pour juice	I do it	man ride bike
Sally kiss baby	Mark hit me	you hide shoe
I eat cereal	boy watch TV	I find shoe
Mom wash dish	hammer hit board	you hug bear

Location Words Added

Dad run *here*	you push swing *up*	knock *on* door
block fall *down*	put foot *on* bar	hide *under* chair
I go *potty*	I hide *under* table	take shoes *off*
throw ball *up*	hide *under* chair	pick *up* toys
put spoon *there*	put rug *on* floor	pull pants *up*
all fall *down*	ball *on* chair	put soap *in* water
we go *home*	put *in* box	Scott talk *on* phone
put shirt *on*	splash *in* water	put hand *in* water
push swing *up*	talk *on* phone	Mum go *to* store
		you go *to* bed

Descriptive Words

comb *your* hair	Mom comb *my* hair	Mom take *little* ball
turn *on* music	I ride *blue* bike	my foot *hurts*
want *more* juice	I pet *soft* kitty	you have *two* cookies
boat go *fast*	I wear *pretty* dress	Mom has *black* purse
my truck *broke*	I want (a) *red* ball	Susie paint *red* house
I have *new* shoes	I want *orange* juice	I wash *sticky* hands
touch *cold* ice	I see (a) *big* truck	I have *clean* face
car go *boom*	I see *my* glasses	

7. Advanced language skills

Add "ing" to action verbs

sitt*ing*	work*ing*	go*ing*
play*ing*	rid*ing*	swimm*ing*
jump*ing*	watch*ing* TV	

Pronouns +

I love you	I'm mad
I'm sad	I'm hungry

Articles

a and the

Other useful phrases

You're welcome	I love you	Fine
Lemme do it	I'm mad, sad, happy	Please
I did it	Thank you	Watch me
Where ball go?	How are you?	I'm hungry

Questions: What?, Where?

What's that?	Where is the girl going?
What does the boy do?	Where's the ball?
Where's that?	

Questions: How?, Why?

How do you make that?	Why is the girl crying?
Why is the boy laughing?	

Negative Phrases: Can't, Don't

I can't	I don't want to
The boy can't go	I don't want water
The girl can't run	

Is

John is a big boy	This is my book

Plural form

ball*s*	I love apple*s*	Mom bakes cookie*s*
dog*s*	see the bird*s*	blow the bubble*s*

This is my book

CHAPTER FIVE

Games for Fun and Learning

**"YOU are the best game in town and
the best toy in the house"**

Dr. Monte Bail, parent and psychiatrist

...DOWN came the RAIN and WASHED the spider OUT...

This chapter is about:

- the special pleasures and rewards of playing games with our children.

- knowing how far our children have matured in their ability to play, so we can plan games that they will enjoy and learn from.

- the many games we can play with our children and the communication skills they can learn by playing.

Where There is Life, There are Games!

1. People games

A child's capacity to play is evident right from birth. The fun comes from being with people — first mom and dad, later brothers and sisters, and then other children. In the beginning, it is the games we play with our child that don't involve anything but the two of us that are often the most fun and that involve natural communication.

The sometimes silly, spontaneous, fun games that we make up to play with our children are especially delightful because they include the tender tickles and reassuring touches that our child loves and needs.

Children who are slow to respond or have difficulty playing with toys, for whatever reason, often miss the social contact that encourages an interest in communication, and the physical contact they need to feel special. Games without toys give them opportunities and encouragement that they might otherwise miss.

People games such as "peek-a-boo", "pat-a-cake" and "gonna getcha" are our child's introduction to the lifelong pleasure of social interaction — interaction which provides pleasure simply because another person is there to share the experience. These games are a way of sharing even when our child has only a limited ability to respond.

Playing a game with our child that involves just the two of us has the added advantage of nothing to break, nothing to clean up, no time wasted wondering where it is, how it works, or where the missing parts are.

Early social games help our child learn because:
- *they have a specific way of being played, with simple roles for both partners*
- *they use only a few actions, sounds, words and sentences*
- *they are very repetitive, and so are predictable*
- *they help our child understand the basis of communication — who does what, what happens, and when his turn will be.*

2. Games with toys and objects

Toys can be anything — any object that a child will be happier playing with pots and pans and other household objects than with store-bought toys.

Games are more than you'll find in a box

Eric's mom: *"The day the groceries get delivered is always a big day in our house. Not because of the food, but because of the boxes that the food is delivered in. Once, we made a fleet of boats, and other times we made a train, a house, a rocket ship, a sink and a stove. The possibilities are endless!"*

Games that grow out of daily activities are especially suited to learning because the words associated with such activities are used frequently. Washing the car, making the beds, sorting the laundry, cleaning mirrors and setting the table are all household chores that can become games if we let our children join in.

How the Ability to Play Develops

*A child's ability to take turns develops and **changes gradually.**
Having realistic expectations of our child's ability to take turns
ensures that the game continues and that we both enjoy it.*

*The scenarios below will help us recognize how our child develops
the ability to take part in play.*

At first

**Our child's turn is any reaction to us as we play
games like "gonna getcha", "peek-a-boo", and
"pat-a-cake".**

When we smile, talk, or play with our child, she
will look, smile, kick, wriggle or vocalize. She
may get upset if we interrupt the interaction that
she is enjoying.

Then

**Our child's sounds and body language let us
know that she anticipates what is coming next
and that she wants to continue the game.** For
example, if we bounce our child on our lap and then
stop, she will bounce to tell us to do it again. Or she
may smile excitedly and pull our hand just before
the "We all fall down" in "Ring around the Rosie".

If we don't respond, our child will persist in her
efforts to let us know that she wants the fun to
continue.

Later

Our child starts the game and expects us to respond by using a sound, word or action related to the game. She can now take on the role that we used to play and start the game herself. For example, she hides her eyes to start the "Peek-a-boo" game or holds out her hand and says "Row, Row" to tell us to sing "Row, Row Your Boat" with her. She now knows when to take her turn in the game.

And still later

Up until now, our child has been able to focus on only one thing at a time. She has been totally absorbed with her toe, her teddy bear, or the person playing with her.

Now our child is developing the ability to shift her focus from the object she is interested in to the person she is playing with and back again. This is a significant step! When our child does develop this ability to shift her focus, she is then more open to absorbing from us the language she needs to learn — language that enables her to be able to understand and talk.

Toys are used in many games, but for our child, the fun and benefit of these games is gained from interacting with us. We really are the best toy in the house!

When we play the 3a way, we create those wonderful opportunities to give our child something to say, a need for saying it and the encouragement and satisfaction to continue to try.

Your Child and Games — 3 Checklists

1. Play with people

Checking the statements below that describe your child will help you:

- recognize the importance of each step your child takes toward learning to communicate
- gain realistic expectations of what your child can do
- plan play that your child will enjoy and learn from

At first, **a child responds and then imitates:**

___ smiles in response

___ enjoys being swung, lifted in play

___ imitates tongue movements

___ continues a sound or action when adult imitates

___ shows his enjoyment for "peek-a-boo" and other nursery rhymes by his attentiveness and body movements

___ imitates patting a toy or rattling a spoon in a cup

___ copies play sounds — animal noises like "moo"

Then, **the child begins to initiate, anticipate and take turns with adults:**

___ offers a toy and hands it over

___ imitates games like "pat-a-cake"

___ likes to be shown books

___ gestures or vocalizes in anticipation of familiar routines in a game

___ copies adult actions with toys

___ takes his turn in "throwing games" with one other person

___ waits for his turn in group games

Later, **the child plays with others:**

___ plays near other children but doesn't join in

___ shares toys happily with another child

___ joins in group games like "catch the ball"

___ follows the rules of simple games

Adapted from "Let's Play" by Roy McConkey

2. Play with toys and objects

Children are not born knowing about things around them. They slowly begin to explore, to learn and to develop an increased capacity for play.

Checking the statements below will help you recognize the value of each stage of play and to plan play activities that your child will enjoy and learn from.

***At first,* a child looks at and then explores objects:**

____ watches and follows a dangling toy moved in front of her face

____ grasps and holds toys

____ mouths toys

____ shakes toys — hits them against the floor, the table

____ examines toys — turns them round in her hand

____ feels objects or rubs them against her hand/ face or bangs them on the table or on the floor to produce a noise

____ drops and/or throws objects and watches what happens

____ squeezes, stretches or tears objects and listens to the sounds they make

***Then,* the child begins to use toys and objects in the ways intended.** She also explores the relationship between two objects and becomes interested in causing things to happen:

____ empties things out or takes things off

____ tries to pull or open parts of toys

____ bangs things which are meant to be banged

____ opens books instead of tearing them

____ pushes or pulls toys that have wheels

____ stacks blocks and rings, or shoes and cushions

____ opens and closes doors

____ puts blocks in a wagon, filling as well as emptying

____ knows how wind-up toys work but needs help in winding them

____ examines small objects

____ loves looking in cupboards, drawers and boxes

____ begins to match things, first by size, then by shape; for example, first a puzzle board with 6 ducks of different sizes and then a puzzle with different shaped pieces

***Later,* the child discovers more abstract "cause and effect" relationships.** She is able to manipulate construction toys with more skill:

____ knows how to work light switches, taps, and the TV converter

____ likes to activate wind-up or pop-up toys

____ plays with toys which link together

____ builds blocks or structures with many pieces

____ experiments with sand, water or playdough

____ begins to scribble or bang with a crayon

____ attempts puzzle boards with many pieces

____ throws and kicks a ball but doesn't catch yet

3. "Pretend play"

Children start to pretend in play when their play skills are fairly well developed and they are beginning to understand what's happening around them. Children who are good at pretending are likely to be better at learning language.

Knowing how well your child is able to pretend will help you join the pretend play in a way that your child can enjoy and learn from.

Checking the statements below will help you recognize the level of pretend play your child will enjoy.

At first, **a child pretends by herself with a single toy or object; she does not involve you:**

___ pushes a toy train across the floor
___ hugs her teddy bear
___ bangs a toy hammer
___ drinks from an empty cup
___ pushes her stroller around

Then, **the child begins to include you in her play, combines two toys or objects when she pretends, and starts to mimic chores she's seen you do around the house:**

___ offers you a bite of her cookie
___ brushes your hair
___ gives you her doll to hug
___ offers you the toy telephone

___ sits her teddy bear on a chair
___ feeds her teddy bear with a bottle
___ tries to sweep the kitchen floor with a broom
___ wants to stand with you at the sink to "help" with the dishes

Later, **the child's pretend play becomes more elaborate as she carries out a sequence of events; she also pretends that one object is something else:**

___ stirs pretend food in a pan, offers it to her teddy bear, and washes up
___ puts a hat on her doll, puts the doll in the stroller and takes her for a walk
___ gets into a cardboard box and pretends to "go for a ride"
___ puts her hand to her ear and pretends to "talk on the phone"
___ builds a simple structure with "Duplo" and pretends it's a car
___ uses a paper towel and pretends it's a blanket for her teddy bear

Still later, **the child takes on roles of people or storybook characters who are favorites of hers, and re-enacts personal experiences which have really impressed her:**

___ plays "house" and is the "mommy"
___ puts on your shoes and pretends to be you
___ gets a bag and pretends to be shopping
___ plays "doctor" with her older brother using a play doctor kit
___ after a pony ride, pretends to ride around on a hobby horse
___ pretends to be a monster from a story she's heard

Sources: C. Westby
             A. Weatherby
             R. McConkey
             L. McCormick & R. Schiefelbush

Games are More Than You'll Find in a Box

The games we can play with our children are limited only by our imagination.

During play, a child learns many skills that will help him deal with life's challenges. In addition to motor skills and problem-solving skills, a child learns to communicate while playing.

When we **adapt the game** to share it with our child, **add language and experience** to help our child learn, and **allow our child to lead**, we create the relaxed, happy time during which our child can learn to:

- focus his attention
- imitate actions and sounds
- take turns
- anticipate what comes next
- recognize that when something is hidden, it still exists
- understand new words
- say new words
- pretend

While playing, it's important to remember that a child who is learning to communicate needs time to take his turn. Let's be patient. Let's wait with anticipation and wait and wait. Let's give our child a chance.

To give our imaginations a boost, the following pages list games we can play with our children.

Early social games

START WITH...

Pizza, pickle, pumpernickel
My little guy shall have a tickle,
One for his nose
And one for his toes
And one for his tummy
Where the hot dog goes
(Dennis Lee)

Peek-A-Boo!
Hide your face from your child's view when you know he's looking at you. After a few seconds, reappear and say "boo!" The mixture of anxiety and excitement will hold your child's attention.

THEN...
Where Is Bobby?
Take turns hiding from each other (e.g., under a blanket). Encourage your child's imitation of your voice, single words and body movements.

Touch And Tickle
Here are some suggestions of people games that are easy and fun to play:

Criss Cross, applesauce
Spiders crawling up your back,
One here, one there,
Now they're crawling in your hair,
Tight squeeze,
Cool breeze,
Now you've got the shivereez!

Catch-me games

START WITH...
Gonna Getcha!
As your child creeps away, crawl after him and catch him, ending with a tickle, a hug. Wait for your child's response; then repeat the game.

THEN...
Come
Similar to "Gonna Getcha" except you wait for a cue from your child before you catch him (e.g., turning around and looking at you; waving to you to come). Later your child might want to catch you.

LATER...
Hide-And-Go-Seek
Help your child hide under a blanket, in a box, behind a sofa. Then pretend you can't find him, saying "Where is ___?" Your joy at seeing your child again — "Oh, there you are!" -— will delight him and encourage him to keep playing the game. Eventually you change roles. You get to hide and your child finds you.

Games with water

START WITH...
Bathing
While bathing your child, imitate her movements and sounds.

THEN...
Grasping The Floating Toy
Allow the toy to float within your child's reach. Encourage your child to reach and grasp it.

LATER...
Floating Toy Game
While bathing your child, play hide-and-go-seek with a toy, splash with it, run it across the water's surface, put it under the water, etc. Encourage your child's varied use of the toy in the water.

Bubbles In A Glass
Show your child how to blow through a straw and make bubbles. Wait for her to respond and encourage her to try to blow them herself.

STILL LATER...
Washing Dishes
Your child may want to imitate you directly by "helping" you wash the dishes. Or you may want to set up a special "sink" with "dirty dishes" for him to wash.

Pour The Water
Find different size containers in which to pour water. You and your child experiment with pouring the water and stopping before it overflows.

Doing What Mom Does
Encourage your child to pretend to do various things that she sees you do regularly (e.g., "pretend" washing and wiping).

Games with balls

AT FIRST...
Grasping The Ball
Roll the ball near your child's body. Be sure that he sees it. Wait for him to retrieve it. (It helps to sit opposite your child with your legs wide apart to contain the ball.)

THEN...
Roll The Ball
Try using the ball in different ways and have your child imitate you. Bounce it, roll it, throw it, carry it, or twirl it. Then you imitate what your child does with the ball.

LATER...
Over The Rope
Take turns throwing or bouncing the ball over and under a rope, while saying: "over", "under", "up", "down", etc.

Where did it go?

START WITH...
Hold The Toy

Find a toy that is easy for your child to grasp. Place it near your child's hand so that he can reach and grasp it. Talk about what it is and if it makes a funny sound.

THEN...
Where Is It?

First get your child's attention by putting a favorite toy within his view. Then move it away. Encourage your child to watch the toy as it is being moved. Remember to name the toy and talk about what's happening. Repeat the game.

LATER...
Find It!

Put a toy within your child's view, and then let it drop to the floor or hide it under something. Encourage your child to find the hidden toy. Say "ah-oh" or "boom" when the toy is dropped, then "Where's the ___?" and "You found the ____". Now it's your child's turn to hide the toy from you.

Games with blocks

START WITH...
I'll Try This!

Let your child play with blocks. If he mouths, bangs, drops, or throws one, you follow his lead — imitate him — and wait for his response. After you have had a game of taking turns, show him other ways to use the blocks.

THEN...
Put Them In The Bucket

Take turns with your child putting blocks in a bucket. After they are all in, dump them out, and repeat the sequence.

Stacking Blocks

Stack several blocks, and then wait to see if your child will do the same.

LATER...
This Is A Car

Use the blocks to build cars, bridges or houses. Encourage your child to help you and then to build his own. Ask your child about what he is doing.

Building A Bridge

Suggest to your child that you and he build something, such as a bridge. Then plan together what each of you will have to do and get before you actually "build". Focus on logically sequencing the steps.

Fun with food

START WITH...
Pudding Picture

Put some pudding in a large pan with a raised edge on it (e.g., a cookie sheet). Put a bib on your child and sit facing her. Encourage your child to explore the pudding with her hands. Allow your child to lead and you follow. If she is hesitant, then demonstrate different finger and hand movements, and make fun sounds (e.g., "plop", "whoops", "tap, tap"). Share the fun of messy play!

THEN...

Make A Salad

Encourage your child to help you make the salad for supper. Allow her to do whatever she can — e.g., washing, tearing lettuce, putting cut vegetables in a bowl, pouring dressing, tossing. It's a great opportunity to "share the moment", add information and get supper ready.

LATER...

I Did It Myself!

Prepare a simple set of directions for making food. Use pictures instead of words. Provide as little help as possible when your child is making the food. Suggested foods: chocolate milk; trail mix; toast; peanut butter sandwich; cereal with milk. Be an enthusiastic audience and commentator!

A Pretend Tea Party

Invite a few favorite dolls and stuffed animals to join you and your child in a tea party. Provide non-breakable dishes and other accessories. Encourage pretend play and imagination.

What is it? Where is it?

START WITH...

What Do You Hear?

Help your child become aware of household sounds by letting him ring the doorbell, dial the phone, turn on the tap, turn on the radio, knock on the door, listen to the clock, etc. Then blindfold him and lead him around the house to hear these sounds. Ask him to identify each one. You can tape familiar sounds and play the tape for your child to identify the sounds. Then you put on a blindfold, and your child leads you around the house to hear these sounds. Prompt him to ask "What's that?"

THEN...

What Is It?

Show your child two objects which are quite different from each other. Say their names, and then blindfold him. Let him handle one object. Ask him "What is it?" If necessary, give him the words.

You can also use two different sounds. Show him two objects and what they sound like. Then blindfold your child and ask him to guess what made that sound. Make up several sets (e.g., a spoon stirring in a bowl and paper tearing; a jar opening and a purse snapping shut; a door opening and water running, etc.).

Then reverse roles. Let your child blindfold you and you guess the sounds.

What's Missing?

Show your child two or more items, and then blindfold him. Remove one item and then let him look and tell you what is missing. Then reverse roles.

LATER...

Blind Man's Bluff

Invite a few children to join in the game. Blindfold the one who is "it". Establish the size of space to stay within and the rules for touching each other.

When the "blind man" touches another player, he becomes "it". Encourage conversation during the game (e.g., "Come and get me", "Where are you?", "I touched you!", "Crawl on the floor", etc.).

Scavenger hunt

START WITH...
Hide And Find Them

Select a few items and show them to your child. Then hide them around your yard or in the house. As your child is looking, help him remember what he is looking for by saying, "Where is the hat?" Once each item is found, have a conversation about it.

THEN...
Find Old Favorites

Name a few favorite items, and then go on a walk to look for them (within the house or outside). When you find each item, say the word and wait for your child to imitate you.

Card games

START WITH...
Give Me The Apple

Paste some magazine pictures onto old playing cards or small pieces of cardboard. Lay out a few cards with the pictures on them and say, "Give me the banana". Try to choose pictures of things that the child knows (e.g., fruit, animals, clothes, furniture, toys, etc.).

There Is A ...

Choose a few words that you want to work on with your child and find pictures of these words. Attach them to cardboard cards. Look at each one with your child and talk about it.

Make The Animal Sound

Using cards that have pictures of animals on them, have your child make the sound of the animal she chooses (e.g., "oink-oink"). If she makes the sound correctly, she gets the card.

THEN...
Lotto

Each player has a card with pictures on it. You hold up a card and ask "Who has the ___?" Explain to your child that if she has the same picture, she can cover it with your card. The winner is the first to cover all of her pictures with matching cards.

Go Fish

Have your child ask for the card she wants from you. If you don't have the card she requests, have her take one more card from the centre pile.

Concentration

Lay out a few matching cards so that your child can see the pictures. Then turn them face down slowly, one by one. Go first, by turning over one card, and then another. Ask, "Do they match?" Wait for her reply. If they do match, take them. If they don't, turn them over again. Then let your child take her turn, prompting her when necessary.

Dice Games

Once your child throws the dice, have her move her figurine (for whatever board game is being used) its allotted number of spaces. Encourage her verbalizations, such as: "I need one more"; "It's my turn"; "Shake the dice"; "Take your move".

LATER...
Telling A Story

Use picture cards or photos that describe a sequence of events, such as getting ready for school in the morning, sledding down a hill, building a house of bl___ _____ _____ your child put the ___ ___ ___ ___ are stories about

(Copyright Braden and Bergstrom, 1988)

When eschar is present, a pressure ulcer cannot be accurately staged until the eschar is removed.

	Stage I	Stage II	Stage III	Stage IV	Unstageable	DTI
Sensory Perception ability to respond meaningfully to pressure related discomfort.	**1. Completely limited:** Unresponsive (does not moan, flinch or gasp) to painful stimuli, due to diminished level of consciousness or sedation, OR limited ability to feel pain over most of the body surface.	**2. Very limited:** Responds only to painful stimuli. Cannot communicate discomfort except by moaning or restlessness OR has sensory impairment which limits the ability to feel pain or discomfort over 1/2 of body.		**3. Slightly limited:** Responds to verbal commands but cannot always communicate discomfort or need to be turned, OR has some sensory impairment which limits the ability to feel pain or discomfort in 1 or 2 extremities.		**4. No impairment:** Responds to verbal commands. Has no sensory deficit which would limit ability to feel or voice pain or discomfort.
Moisture degree to which skin is exposed to moisture	**1. Constantly moist:** Skin is kept moist almost constantly by perspiration, urine, etc. Dampness is detected every time patient is moved or turned.	**2. Very moist:** Skin is often but not always moist. Linen must be changed at least once a shift.		**3. Occasionally moist:** Skin is occasionally moist, requiring and extra linen approximately once a day.		**4. Rarely moist:** Skin is usually dry; linen only requires changing at routine intervals.

— your child's ___ materials and ___ grasped and ___ ply.

Can I___ _____ ck?

___ ____ ___ article of clothing and experiment with your child! Explore the different movements that can be used (e.g., throwing, dropping, waving, pulling, etc.).

LATER...
It's Time For ...

Choose a few situations where you know your child connects a certain item of clothing with a specific activity (e.g., a bib and eating, a coat and going outside, pajamas and going to bed, etc.). Be consistent in naming the activity and the associ-

ated item. Then wait for your child to complete the sentence (e.g., "Here's your pajamas. It's time for ___.").

Doing The Laundry

Have your child help you sort the clothes, load the washing machine, and turn the machine on; use simple one-word phrases for him to imitate.

Put Your Clothes Away

After you have done the laundry, have your child help put his clothes away. Help him by pointing and giving him simple directions.

Dress The Doll

Ask your child to choose various items of clothing and put them on a doll. Gradually increase the number of choices your child has to choose from (start with 2 items).

STILL LATER...
Dress Mom

Allow your child to attempt dressing you (e.g., putting your gloves on). Other skills can be included, such as combing hair.

LATER YET...
Doll Play

While playing with the doll, encourage your child to get her doll ready for bed (e.g., have your child name each item while undressing the doll. You can then suggest bathing it, combing its hair, putting it to bed, etc.). Encourage conversation throughout the doll play.

Touching

Select various textures of material scraps. Let your child touch with his fingers or rub the textures against his face. Tell him how each thing feels (e.g., soft, rough, wet, dry, etc.) Then blindfold him and ask him to identify the piece that you give him or touch his face with. Whenever you play a blindfold game, take turns and have your child blindfold you.

FINALLY...
Dress Up

Give your child old clothes to try on. Have conversations about what she is wearing, where she is going, who she is, etc.

Here Is Your Bag Of Clothes

Give everyone in the family a bag of clothes. Tell each one to find and put on his hat, a shoe, a glove, etc. Make the combinations of clothing amusing (e.g., one boy could have mother's hat, father's shoes and the baby's bib). Discuss the funny clothing everyone has put on and make sure to point to each piece of clothing you're talking about.

Play going to the store

Bring Me A Hat

Display the items "for sale" on the table but limit the number of items to those your child recognizes. Show the "store" to your child and ask him if he wants to do some "shopping" for you. Ask him to bring you one of the items and give him a paper bag to put it in. If he brings you the correct item, tell him what a great shopper he is.

Who Has It?

Each participant is given a bag containing several items. The leader asks for a certain item and takes it from the person who has it. The first person to have an empty bag is the winner.

I Want The Doll

Assemble several articles: food, clothing, toys, household items, etc. Have your child choose something by any means he can (verbal or otherwise). Observe how he lets you know what he wants, and then interpret, saying it as he would if he could. Expand on the topic.

Matching games

Pictures And Objects

Using magazine pictures of furniture, household objects, clothing, etc., let your child match the appropriate picture to the actual object in your home and have her imitate or say the word. Gradually increase the number of pictures you use.

Animal Sounds And Pictures

Point to the picture of an animal and then make its sound. Wait for your child to imitate you. Or make the animal sound first and then point to the picture. Wait again for her response. After awhile, your child may attempt a sound if you just point to a picture.

Sorting games

START WITH...
Put Them Here

Keep a collection of similar items and have your child sort them according to size, color, length or weight. (Some will be easier than others.) Use such items as buttons, beads, stones, shells, crayons, or shoes. Label the items and add information about them.

THEN...
How I Look When I'm Angry

Show your child drawings of faces that are happy, sad, crying, laughing, angry, smiling, coughing, scared, surprised. Demonstrate different looks with your own face. Then ask your child to show you the picture of the face that matches yours.

Weather Chart

Cut out pictures of various types of weather conditions. Tape them to the front door. Each day, let your child look outside at the weather and then find the appropriate picture, while you tell her what the weather is like. (Use only a few pictures at the beginning.)

Fun naming things

START WITH...
I Know The Names!

Think of a few items in your house that your child uses every day. Go around the house, touch each item and say its name. Wait for your child to imitate you by touching or by saying the word.

THEN...
Show Me The Dog

Using a set of simple pictures, take turns with your child pointing to the picture of the object you name.

Pick a theme

Apple Week

Choose a theme as the focus of many different activities (e.g., "apples"). You can buy apples, pick apples in an orchard, make applesauce, make up a story about apples, use words that relate to apples (e.g., "bite", "red", "hard", "core", etc.).

Puzzles

START WITH...

It's easier to begin with puzzles that have inset pieces of whole objects. Encourage your child to take out and explore the puzzle pieces. You can label and comment on what your child is interested in and what he does with the pieces.

Early on, your child may just want to dump the pieces out and then let you put them in. Then he might enjoy using the puzzle pieces as toys. You can expand on the game by making the actions or sounds the puzzle pieces might make.

THEN...
You Found The Arm

Use a puzzle of a human figure which has separate puzzle pieces for each body part. Ask your child what piece he wants to pick up and then talk about it as you help him place it in the puzzle. Wait for him to pick up another piece.

LATER...
Learning Puzzle Language
With a more difficult puzzle, model for your child the appropriate phrases that describe what is happening:

"another one"

"puzzle piece"

"Where does this one go?"

"Turn it around"

"Does it fit?"

"The corner pieces"

"The straight pieces"

Show Me How You____"
Ask your child how he runs, jumps, sleeps, sits, throws a ball, turns the page, bangs the table, drinks milk, etc. You can imitate, label, expand and applaud!

LATER...
Stand Next To Me
This is a good game for teaching prepositions. One person gives directions, while the others follow:

"Mom, stand in *front* of the fridge."

"Dave, stand *next* to Phillip."

And so forth.

Follow me

START WITH...
Do This
Ask your child to do what you do. Then switch roles and let your child initiate and you follow his lead. If he initiates by moving a certain way, you follow him! Concentrate on body movements that make noise (e.g., clap hands, stamp feet, rub hands, tap fingers or feet, scratch etc.)

THEN...
In The Car
Use a simple sound to initiate the repetitive movement of the wipers (sh-sh) and turn signals (k-k) and encourage your child to imitate them.

Stop-and-go games

You and your child can move around the room (e.g., hopping, running, skipping, twirling, walking, etc.) until either one of you says "Stop". No one moves until your child lets you know he wants to "Go". Repeat the sequence.

When we think about playing games with our children, most of us automatically think about toys that will interest them. But toys for young children are just a small part of play and, initially, not the most important in helping them learn to communicate. With toys, or without, it's how WE play the games with our children that can make learning fun.

CHAPTER SIX

Moving Forward with Music

"Without music, life would be a mistake."
Friedrich Nietzsche, philosopher

This chapter is about:

- the magic of music and how it can make learning easy and fun.

- adapting the words or actions of songs to encourage our children to join in.

- making up our own words to familiar tunes so our songs have more meaning for our children.

The Magic of Music

Every parent has watched in wonder as a lullaby, a hug and a gentle rocking motion turn a screaming infant into a sleeping angel. Even before they are born, babies respond to and are comforted by the steady heartbeat and rocking motions of their mothers' bodies. And after birth, rhythm continues to be a comfort.

Children learn to respond to music very early and soon begin to involve themselves by moving their bodies and swaying; later by imitating rhythms and sounds.

Through music activities, children learn pre-language skills naturally— listening, paying attention and concentrating — which lead to anticipating what comes next and being able to follow directions. All these things form the foundation for learning conventional communication. The magic of music comes from sharing music activities which encourage:

- physical contact
- repetition
- taking turns
- non-verbal responses
- vocal play
- action as well as speech
- an awareness of the appropriate timing for action and /or words

In addition, music has advantages over other play activities. The rhythm and melody of the music help our child to anticipate and recognize when it's his turn. As he becomes more experienced, he will be ready to take his turn. This "timing" is a very important conversational skill. Music really is special in helping our children move forward. We can create music whenever the spirit moves us. It can be done anywhere and anytime — in the bath, in the car, or wherever you are!

Adapting to Share Music

"Don't worry if it's not good enough for anyone else to hear"

Let's not worry if we don't have a voice like Barbra Streisand — our child will not be critical of tone, key and range. She will respond to the rhythm of our speech and the love and affection with which we sing to her.

If we're feeling hesitant about singing, we can begin with the songs we know well, the ones our mother sang to us, or with rhymes that we can recite in a singsong voice. By trying different types of songs, we'll soon find out what we're most comfortable singing.

We can expand our repertoire by asking our child's teacher what songs our child sings in school, listening to children's programs on radio and TV, buying children's records or borrowing recordings from libraries.

"Slow down, you move too fast"

Our child can learn many more actions and words if we sing slowly and at her speed. This means slowing down and enunciating very clearly, so that our child has a chance to hear the words. Then, when she begins to anticipate the actions or sounds, the slower pace gives our child the opportunities to sing her part.

> **Katie's Mom:** *"There's always joy when there's feedback. The first joy came when we knew that Katie recognized the song. Then she started doing the motions along with us and then filling in the words. We learned to SLOW DOWN the songs. We slowed down so that she could really hear the words that she knew. Another thing we learned is that repetition is VERY important. Probably four or five times more repetition than we thought!"*

We can't expect our partner to know what to do the second time we sing a song, but if we keep repeating, giving her chances and letting her know what is expected, our child will take a turn when she's ready.

Initially we'll be "The Entertainer", providing all the music, actions and the words; then we'll be "The Director", helping our child do the motions. After many repetitions, we'll be "The Responsive Partner" and adapt the music activity to encourage our child to take an active part. We'll wait to allow her to take her turn.

"It's the singer, not the song"

If we can't think of a song that fits perfectly with the communication goal we've chosen for our child, let's make up a song. We can start with a familiar tune, and then change the words to fit the situation. "Here We Go Round The Mulberry Bush" can become "This Is The Way We Wash Our Hands", "Eat Our Supper", or "Walk To School". "Jesus Loves Me This I Know" can become "On The Table Put A Spoon."

We can make music a part of our child's day from morning till night:

- brushing teeth
- riding in the car
- going to the potty
- going for a walk
- having a bath
- washing hands
- going to bed
- getting dressed
- eating
- climbing the stairs
- changing diapers
- going to child care

Our adaptations of songs are limited only by our imagination. The copyright department will never catch us! If we can find the child-like, fun place within ourselves from which to sing, our children will recognize it and join in. Let's take liberties as did Katie's mom, who found travelling in the car a great time for communicating, even before her children were able to respond:

Katie's Mom: *"Travelling in the car gives me a perfect chance to turn off the radio (and tape machine). I use this time (captive in a relatively small metal box with my kids) to sing songs with them at our own tempo. We reinforce the songs we've done at home. It's also a great time for Katie's younger brothers and I to enjoy just being together and 'communicating' — hearing our voices.*

"We repeat songs over and over and over (particularly when I am the only adult in the car!), and the children love it.

Here is an example of a funny little song we made up in the car. It has endless verses, and it all started on a bumpy road...

> Bumpy road, bumpy road
> BUMPY, BUMPY
> Bumpy road, bumpy road
> BUMPY, BUMPY

"The refrain is BUMPY, BUMPY, *and the kids suggested all the verses:*

> Big tree, big tree   Windy day, windy day
> BUMPY, BUMPY   BUMPY, BUMPY
> Big tree, big tree   Windy day, windy day
> BUMPY, BUMPY   BUMPY, BUMPY

"Then we tried friends and relatives:

> Uncle Bob, Uncle Bob
> BUMPY, BUMPY
> Uncle Bob, Uncle Bob
> BUMPY, BUMPY."

When we make up songs on the spot to describe what's happening, it doesn't matter whether or not they rhyme, whether or not the melody is real — kids love them!

To the tune of "London Bridge is Falling Down"

Tyler's bridge is falling down
Falling down
Falling down
Tyler's bridge is falling down
Mo – mmy'll fix it!

To the tune of "Jingle Bells"

Hat on head
Hat on head
Hat on Katie's head
Oh, what fun it is to wear
A hat on Katie's head!

Guidelines for writing a song

• Choose a simple, familiar tune (e.g., a nursery rhyme, a TV jingle, a song from a tape of children's music)

• Make sure there are less than 10 different key words in the song

• Use words which relate to the people, objects and actions your child knows

• Think of how your child can use actions and gestures in the song

• Decide which props will be needed

• Think of how to adapt the song so your child can participate.

"Let's get physical"

As in all play, the best interactions take place when we're close together and facing each other, so that our child sees the action at the same time as hearing the words that describe the action. This richness of information helps our child understand, remember, and later use the new gestures or words.

Many of the songs our children love best involve simple actions; therefore songs or rhymes that involve actions like "Row, row, row your boat" or "Pat-a-Cake" are a good place to start.

Adapting to share the music with our child means matching sensitively the music activity with our child's energy level. Playing "Ring Around the Rosie" when our child is tired isn't a great idea. A gentle lullaby that recognizes how he is feeling does wonders for him. Words that we add at this time will be heard.

"You...nobody but you"

Much of what our children are exposed to on TV is fast paced. Most children's programs jump quickly from one topic to another, and the graphics, voices and actions are all very fast. This can be overwhelming for a child and encourages the habit of tuning out. Radio, which is seldom child-oriented, also encourages the habit of tuning out in children.

We want to expose our children to sounds and images that they can comfortably absorb and assimilate, to help them make sense of their world, not tune out. So let's turn off the radio and turn off the TV, and let's turn on our children by making music together.

Although our child gets pleasure from the rhythm of recordings, the experience won't be as successful for learning to communicate as when we do the singing together because we can slow down and:

- **a**dapt the song to share it with our child
- **a**dd language and experience to help our child learn
- **a**llow our child to lead.

A Child's Response to Music Changes as She Matures

The statements below describe how a child learns to take a more active part in musical activities. Please check (√) the statements that best describe your child. This will help you choose songs and games that your child will enjoy and from which she will learn.

At first

_____ When I start singing, my child reacts. If she's upset, she might calm down. When she's calm, her face lights up or she may start to make sounds.

_____ When I turn on a music box or musical mobile suspended over her bed, my child becomes quiet and looks to find the sound.

_____ When we are face to face and I stop singing, my child may wriggle or smile, or look at me, or make a sound as if to say, "Let's do it again".

Then

_____ My child loves songs with actions, which, at first, I gently help him do — e.g., clapping, kicking, banging on an instrument, rocking back and forth, falling down.

_____ When I stop and wait, my child may vocalize as well as imitate a simple action I have just done.

> "If you're happy and you know it, CLAP your hands"
> "The wheels on the bus go ROUND and ROUND"

_____ In songs which we have practised many times, my child begins to anticipate his turn in the song — e.g., when I sit with my child face to face on my knees, and begin to recite "HUMPTY DUMPTY sat on the wall", he may wriggle or squeal in anticipation of the "BIG FALL".

_____ When I sing or when music comes on the stereo, my child may begin to bounce up and down, as if trying to dance.

Later

_____ In songs which are becoming familiar to my child, she tries to fill in the sounds, words or actions which come at the end of the line.

> I sing: "Old MacDonald had a farm".
> My child sings: "AAAy ay ay" — her attempt at "E-I-E-I-O!"

> I sing: "Head and Shoulders, Knees and..."
> My child sings: "doe" — meaning "toe" — and reaches for her toes.

_____ In songs which I have paired with daily routines, my child begins to make the association as soon as she hears the song.

> I sing: "This is the way we WASH OUR HANDS". My child runs over to the sink.

> I sing: "The water is fine, fine, fine...It's my..." My child sings: "Ba da" —
> meaning "Bathtime" — and heads for the bathroom.

_____ When I ask my child, "Do you want a song?" or "Music?", she may use a gesture to indicate a song she has in mind, or run and select a favorite recording.

Still later

_____ My child is beginning to gain control of his singing voice as he fills in parts of the song.

_____ My child can fill in more than one word when I stop and wait in the middle of a line.

> I say: "Put it in the oven for ..." (Pat-a-cake rhyme)
> My child says: "Baby'n me."

_____ When playing by himself or lying awake in bed, my child sings familiar favorites to himself. The words aren't all there, and the tune wouldn't win a Juno award, but I can usually recognize the song.

_____ My child will come and ask me to sing or play a song. He might bring me a record or a prop we have used for a particular song. Or he might tell me by singing a small part of the song, or saying the title or a key word from the song.

> My child comes out of the blue with: "Picnic".
> I take a minute to figure it out: "Oh, you want Teddy Bear's Picnic?"

> My child brings me a little stick and begins to blow. I respond :"Oh, you're blowing the candle. Shall we sing Happy Birthday?" His face lights up in agreement.

_____ Sometimes when he overhears me talking, my child will relate a word or phrase I used with a song he knows, and then burst into song.

> I say to someone: "There's a full moon tonight".
> My child starts singing: "In the evening underneath the moon" (a line from the song "Skinnymarink").

Children do not grow tired of favorite simple songs as they progress to enjoying more complex ones. The familiarity of an old favorite can give a child confidence to progress to more advanced communication goals, beginning with imitations and actions, and progressing through sounds to words and phrases.

The music suggestions that follow are organized according to levels, but don't take the levels as gospel. If your child enjoys a certain musical toy or activity, encourage him to participate in whatever way he can.

Music Activities

At first

Songs and Rhymes

• As you are relaxing with your child, sing favorite songs to familiarize him with the rhythm, melody and words.

• Play selected music (classical, popular, children's recordings) while sitting and listening together. Watch for and imitate your child's movements and vocal responses to the music.

• Sing a familiar melody, but substitute one or two syllables your child makes for the actual words. After one "verse", pause, so your child can let you know that he wants more by a sound or by a body movement.

"Pat-A-Cake"

Pat-a-Cake, pat-a-cake, baker's man
(clap hands)
Bake me a cake as fast as you can (clap hands)
Roll it and roll it (roll hands) and mark it with a B
And put it in the oven for (Child's name) and me (give child a hug).

You can do the actions yourself or move the child's hands for the actions. Pause when rhyme is over to let child indicate, as in Humpty Dumpty, if he wants more .

Make up simple words to go with a familiar melody. The words should describe an activity you and your child are sharing. For example, to the tune of "The Farmer in the Dell":

Molly drinks her milk
Molly drinks her milk
Molly has a cup of milk
Molly drinks her milk.

Rhymes recited in a sing-song style are also fun. For example, "Washing, washing, washing hair, Mommy washes Jamie's hair."

"Humpty Dumpty"

Humpty Dumpty sat on a wall (sit with your child on your lap).
Humpty Dumpty had a great fall (pretend to let your child fall and bring him up again)
All the king's horses and all the king's men couldn't put Humpty together again.

Once your child is familiar with the rhyme, pause before "fall" and let him anticipate the fall by laughing or body language. Pause after the rhyme to give him a chance to indicate by body language or through vocalization, whether he wants more. You can then interpret this communication verbally — "More!" or "No more".

"This Little Piggy"

> This little piggy went to market
> This little piggy stayed home
> This little piggy had roast beef
> This little piggy had none
> And this little piggy went wee wee wee all the way home.

For each line of the rhyme, wiggle one of your child's fingers or toes. For the last line, run your fingers up to the child's chin and tickle her. Your child can also wiggle her fingers while you recite the rhyme.

"Head And Shoulders, Knees And Toes"

Point to the named body parts on yourself or on your child as you sing.

> Head and shoulders, knees and toes
> Knees and toes, knees and toes,
> Head and shoulders, knees and toes,
>   Eyes, ears, mouth and nose.

"If You're Happy And You Know It"

> If you're happy and you know it, clap your hands (*clap, clap*)
> If you're happy and you know it, clap your hands (*clap, clap*)
> If you're happy and you know it
> And you really want to show it
> If you're happy and you know it, clap your hands. (*clap,clap*)

Variation: You can include a sound your child can say — e.g., "If you're happy and you know it, say 'ba'."

"Jack In The Box"

> Jack in the Box
> Sitting so still
> Won't you come up?
> Yes I will!

Have your child crouch down tightly during the chant. On the last line:

- at first, just encourage him to jump up
- later, he may jump up on his own and may say "up"
- still later, he will jump up and on his own yell "Yes, I will!"

"Ring Around The Rosie"

> Ring around the rosie (*hold hands and walk in a circle*)
> A pocketful of posies
> Hush-a, Hush-a,
> We all fall down. (*fall to the ground*)

Pause before "down" to give your child a chance to initiate by falling down or verbalizing "down".

Rhythm Grab Bag

Instruments You Can Buy

drum
tambourine
xylophone
recorder
kazoo
bells
cymbals
triangle

Instruments You Can Make

pot lids
wooden spoons
metal spoons
jars filled with graduated amounts of water (use as chimes)
various size pots (use as drums)
empty boxes (use as drums)
containers filled with rice or beans (use as shakers)

Place several rhythm instruments on the floor or in a large bag. Each adult and child takes an instrument and experiments with it. Sometimes you play your instruments together and sometimes only one of you plays while the others listen.

Variations for later:
• To choose their instrument, players can use skills ranging from pointing to sentences
• Players can describe what they are doing

Clap To The Music
Accompany singing and recorded music by clapping, stomping and patsching (hitting thighs).
Variation: Use different homemade or purchased instruments for accompaniment.

Find The Music Box
Play the child's favorite music box, hidden close by underneath a blanket or furniture. Allow him to retrieve it. You can make a game of racing to it once you see he has identified the general location.

Then

Hide The Music Box
Played in a similar fashion to "Hide and Seek", you each take turns hiding the music box while the other is out of the room. Finding the box is done by listening for the music. Vocal clues such as "Yes - no; You're hot - you're cold" can be given.

What Made That Noise?
Show the child two items that make very different noises (e.g., a rattle and a pot cover with a stick). Let him make noise with each one. Then have him cover his eyes while you play one of the sound-makers. When he opens his eyes, the child points to or names the sound-maker he heard.

Variation: You can use three, four, or five sound-makers and include some whose sounds are similar.

"Old MacDonald Had A Farm"
Old MacDonald had a farm
E-I-E-I-O
And on this farm he had a cow
E-I-E-I-O

With a moo-moo here, and a moo-moo there
Here a moo, there a moo,
Everywhere a moo-moo
Old MacDonald had a farm
E-I-E-I-O.

When you are singing, pause to encourage your child to fill in sounds in the chorus "E-I-E-I-O". Pause to encourage him to imitate the different animal sounds. As you sing, show him pictures of the farm animals. Later, let your child choose the action or animal you will use in the verse "and on his farm he had a ____".

Make Up A Song

Make up lyrics to familiar melodies or rhythms, using words to encourage your child to understand. Pause before the last word to encourage him to supply the word.

This is the way we brush our teeth,
brush our teeth, brush our ____".

Variations: Songs can be made up to encourage your child to fill in more than one word.

Note: Most children will enjoy having the same verse repeated several times.

Finger Plays

Eensie Weensie spider ran up the water spout
(fingers climb up)
Down came the rain and washed the spider out
(fingers move down like raindrops)
Out came the sun and dried up all the rain
(hands held together above the head)
And the eensie weensie spider ran up the spout
again. *(fingers climb up)*

"If You're Happy And You Know It"

You can now incorporate more complicated actions such as:

- rub your tummy
- shake your head
- touch your eyebrow

Variation: Your child can volunteer the action when you pause (e.g., "If you're happy and you know it, say 'quack, quack'").

"Where Is Thumbkin?"

Where is Thumbkin? Where is Thumbkin?
Here I am. Here I am.
How are you today sir?
Very glad, I thank you.
Run away. Run away.

Additional verses can be sung about Pointer, Middle Man, Ringer and Pinky.

Variations: Sing a song with your child; you sing the first phrase and your child responds; then your child takes the lead and you respond.

Ball Play
Tune: "Mulberry Bush"

This is the way we ...
  • roll the ball
  • kick the ball
  • bounce the ball

"Sing High — Sing Low"
Raise your hands over your head when singing a song in high register.

Put your hands at chest level when singing in a normal register.

Put your hands on floor when singing in a low register. Encourage your child to imitate body movements while you sing in *exaggerated* registers (e.g., falsetto, basso profundo).

Variation: High — stand on a chair or on tiptoes; normal — kneel on the floor; low — lie down flat on the floor.

Echoes
You clap out a one-syllable sound or word and your child echoes. Start with sounds the child knows well. Nonsense words can also be fun. At first his turn may be either a sound or a clap, and later he may combine the sound and clap together. Variation: Try two syllable words or a short phrase (e.g., "How are you?").

Later

Talking Drums
Place a large drum, box or pot between you and your child. Each player beats out his message, talking and drumming at the same time.

e.g., "How are you?" "Fine. "
       X   X   X   X

"How old are you?" "Four."
  X   X   X   X   X

Record Jackets
As you listen to a record with your child, you can talk about the pictures on the record jacket which relate to the songs (e.g., "Who was that song about?")

Old Favorites

Twinkle Twinkle Little Star

Mary Had A Little Lamb

Happy Birthday

The Wheels On The Bus

B-I-N-G-O
Doe, A Deer
Farmer In The Dell
Here We Are Together
He's Got The Whole World In His Hands
If You're Happy And You Know It
London Bridge
Old MacDonald

Oats and Beans and Barley Grow
Rock-A-Bye Baby
Row, Row, Row Your Boat
She'll be Coming Round The Mountain
This Old Man
Where Is Thumbkin?
Yankee Doodle

Sometimes we draw a blank and cannot remember the words to familiar melodies. We can change the words to match our activity (e.g., dressing, painting, playing).

Resources for Parents

BOOKS:

Music For Fun, Music for Learning
Birkenshaw, Lois
Holt-Reinhart & Winston
1974

Your Baby Needs Music: Music and Movement for Infants and Toddlers
Cass-Beggs, Barbara
Addison-Wesley Publishers Ltd.
26 Prince Andrew Place
Don Mills, Ontario M3C 2T8
Second Edition, 1990

What To Do Until The Music Teacher Comes
Glatt, Louise
Brandol Music Ltd.
11 St. Joseph St.
Toronto M4Y 1J8
1978

Eye Winker, Tom Tinker, Chin Chopper:
50 Musical Fingerplays
Glazer, Tom
Zephyr, 1973

Rock-A-Bye Baby
Miller, Carl S.
Unicef

CHAPTER SEVEN

Sharing Books

"What is the use of a book", thought Alice,
"without pictures or conversations?"
Lewis Carroll, author

This chapter is about:

- how we can create unlimited opportunities to help our children discover the wonder, words, and wisdom in books.

- how we can be creative in making reading time a communicating time.

- how we can make up stories and create home-made books that will delight our children and help them learn.

The Riches of Reading

In an often confusing and unpredictable world, books offer our children opportunities to experience objects, actions and events that are clear and constant. And for young children, the experiences, the objects, the people and the happenings in books — are real.

Books are an infinite source for encouraging the development of communication because:

- Looking at books develops concentration and attention span
- Our interested involvement helps our children learn language
- Imitating, labelling, expanding, and taking turns happen naturally while sharing a book with our children
- Reading and rereading a favorite, familiar book will reinforce newly learned words
- We can focus on specific actions, words or concepts by choosing books with these words and concepts, and encouraging our children to find, point at or name the animals, toys, foods, etc.

*Sharing books with our children is an ideal time for having conversations. It's a quiet, cozy time with something to look at and **talk** about — an experience to share.*

Before We Turn the First Page

The experience of sharing books with our children will be all the richer when we take the time to thoughtfully plan the occasion.

Creative beginnings

In the beginning when most children have very little interest in looking at books, creative planning can make a big difference in getting and keeping their attention. We can:

- Begin with "feel", "smell" or "do" books designed to allow a child to participate actively — to touch, smell, zip or button.
- Have familiar objects nearby, like a cup, a pillow, or a hat that are pictured in the book, so that the child can see them and touch them.
- Allow the child to lead — let him turn the pages and choose the pictures he wants to look at.
- Choose books about the child's everyday experiences.

> **Katie's mom:** *"We started at the beginning by showing her pictures of everything we could think of, just to expand Katie's horizons. Now we use books that portray familiar situations to just reinforce what Katie has done in her everyday experiences — a trip to the doctor, a birthday party..."*

Check it out

Before we read a book to our child, it makes sense to check it out first. The best books combine an interesting story told simply with beautiful pictures that enhance the story.

Our child will enjoy and be able to learn more from books that are matched to his level of understanding. The list at the end of this chapter offers some suggestions about books as they relate to progressive levels of development.

Choose a goal

In reading with a purpose, we can help our child learn new words by finding books with those words in them. If we want our child to learn the word "ball", *Belinda's Ball* is a good choice. Watching our child's responses to a favorite book can give us clues as to what actions and words he is interested in and wants to talk about.

Finding the Book

New and used books

The public library is the best place to start looking for books for our child. It offers unlimited opportunities to try out different kinds of books. If a book from the library is a tremendous hit with our child, we should consider buying it because we know it is one she will love and use. Many of the books on the list at the end of this chapter, and other equally good books, come in paperback and are not expensive. As well as bookstores, yard sales and rummage sales are good places to look for books to buy. It is important to have good books around — it encourages the sharing, the fun and the learning that come from reading together.

Recognize favorites

As children develop their individual interests and their preferences begin to emerge, they become more and more determined to choose their own books. It's important to recognize their personal preferences. Some children love Dick Bruna's flat, simplified shapes; others do not find them interesting at all. What bothers one child — for example, a monster figure — will not bother another child. Our preferences are important too. If we really enjoy a book, it's easy to read it enthusiastically with our child.

Write your own story

If we have a specific language goal in mind and can't think of or find a story which includes that goal, we can make up our own story, following the traditional patterns. It may not be as classic as *The Three Bears,* but it can serve a useful purpose and may become a family favorite.

For example, if we want to teach our child to say "in", we might make up a story like this one:

> *Kevin's mittens were on the floor, so Mama put them IN the cupboard.*
> *Kevin's blocks were on the floor, so Mama put them IN the cupboard.*
> *Kevin's books were on the floor, so Mama put them IN the cupboard.*

And so on — with our child suggesting items for Mama to put in the cupboard.

> *Kevin wanted his mittens, so Mama opened the cupboard and everything fell OUT!*

We should try to keep our made-up stories simple so that they are easy to remember and so that the language goal of the story doesn't get lost in a clutter of words.

Make your own books

A home-made book tailored to our child's interests is a winner! All we need is paper, scissors, cardboard, string and glue. Taking two squares of cardboard for the "covers", we punch a hole in the top left corner. We do the same with squares of paper, and when the "book" is finished, we can join the covers and the pages with a piece of string. Our book will lie flat and be easy to open. Each page might have one picture of something our child loves: trucks, animals, things to touch, dolls. Magazines and catalogues are filled with suitable pictures. Stickers on a variety of topics are also available .

> **Jamie's Mom:** *"We began by thinking about Jamie, and so I thought what interests him more than his hands, and so we went through and added in his book, pictures of all the things that interest James — his hands, the vacuum cleaner, trains, etc. He loves trains and now says "trains" consistently from looking at the book."*

A photo album is always fascinating. Children love to look at pictures of family members (themselves especially!) and events which are special. Talking about the pictures, identifying the people, objects and events can provide many hours of enjoyment.

A surprise book. Children who tend to flip through the pages of a book without any apparent interest might like a "surprise" book. A photo album or scrapbook with all the pages blank except for one, on which is pasted a picture of his favorite thing, is a great attention-getter. The picture may be a photo of herself or a likeness of her favorite toy or pet. We can have our child help us add a page — e.g., a tracing of his hand or foot, or a "drawing" of him dressed in his favorite clothes. This is a good start to learning words for body parts and clothing.

To have and to hold

Most of our child's books should be kept where she can get them out easily, sort through them and either "read" them by herself or bring the book to us. When she is just beginning to handle books, we should have ones that she can manage to hold easily, like board books and small size books. A book is something to be used, not protected; so it is important to own books as well as to borrow them from the library.

Reading Together

Spending a special time each day sharing books with our child can become a happy habit.

> **Jason's Mom:** *"The nicest thing about books is that it's our opportunity to be close, and every morning and every night Jason and I share something we both enjoy."*

We can choose a peaceful time and a comfortable spot and position ourselves to face our child. We can **OWL — observe** our child's facial expression and body language and focus of attention. Let's encourage our child to hold the book, turn the page and point. Let's wait and **give him as much time as he needs** to look at the pictures and respond with sounds or words.

> **Cameron's Dad:** *"What I learned in reading with Cameron was to wait so Cameron could let me know what he was interested in and then to follow his lead. That was for me the key — to **follow his lead** as opposed to me initiating."*

Take turns reading

Reading aloud is an excellent time for taking turns. When we pause, our child has the chance to fill in words — "and when she opened the door, she saw a _____!!" With a familiar story in a picture book, we can read one page, our child the next. Our child's contribution will depend, of course, on the level of her language development — it will range from pointing, to saying "moo" for a cow, to a description of what is happening on the page. Our response can add language and information. Being aware of what we say and how we say it can help our child learn.

> **Jordan's Mom:** *"I found that taking turns is really important, but so hard to do. It's so easy to talk for Jordan. It's better to let him talk for himself.*
>
> *"What I find hardest, though, is the waiting when I know that Jordan knows the word or the first part of the word. It's much better to hold back and let him say the word and for me to repeat it back to him so he gets the correct pronunciation. It also sort of establishes for Jordan, 'Yeah, I did say the right word, and Mommy said it back the way I said it. Yeah, I'm right.' It's really reinforcing for Jordan."*

Say it with feeling

It's much more interesting and fun when we read dramatically, emphasizing the rhythm, the rhyme and the words we want our child to learn. When we show anticipation for the next word or the next page, we make a story more exciting. Our child's response to the way we read will tell us if we're doing all right and what parts of the story our child finds most interesting.

Take liberties

Sometimes we can make a book more interesting for our child by changing the name of a character in the book to our child's name or the name of a family member or friend.

We can change the story to fit the circumstances of our child's life. If our child is enjoying a particular page and is getting a great deal out of it, we can stay with that page for a while.

Other less interesting pages can be passed over quickly. It is perfectly all right to read only one or two pages of a book if that serves our purpose or our child's purpose.

If the text of a book is beyond our child's level, we might tell the story in our own words or just talk about what's happening in the pictures.

Over and over again

There are times when a child will want the same book over and over. We can try to introduce others (take turns — "I choose one, then you choose one"), but we should recognize that this particular book is important to the child right now. Let's read it — again and again — with style and flair, of course!

Reading books together is most effective as a way of learning to communicate when we: • adapt the book to share it with our child
• add information and experiences at our child's level
• allow our child to lead

Become a storyteller

Traditional stories like *The Three Bears, The House That Jack Built,* and *The Three Little Pigs* have been told over and over and polished by generations of storytellers. They have been enjoyed by thousands of children and are likely to be a hit with our children too.

When we tell these stories to our children:

• The strong, repetitive, predictable language like "I'll huff and I'll puff and I'll blow your house down" provides many opportunities for our child to participate with words and actions.

• As a storyteller we can tell and retell the story anytime and anywhere! We can look at our children and see how they are responding and participating, and then adjust the story or our style accordingly.

The easiest way to learn a story is to read it in a picture book several times with our child. Then we can rehearse it in our mind before we tell it. We shouldn't hesitate to adapt or shorten a story to suit our child's attention span and her ability to understand and participate.

The fun of these stories is the frequent and consistent repetition. If we stray and say "I'm going to gobble you up" one time and "I'm going to eat you" the next, we miss opportunities for using repetitive language that our child expects and learns from. Consistent repetition helps our child become more involved in the story because she can anticipate what comes next. Besides, our child won't let us deviate too much — children are sticklers for accuracy!

As with reading aloud, it helps to think ahead about the specific actions, sounds, words or phrases that our child can learn to do or say in the story. Telling the story many times so that it becomes familiar helps our child anticipate the key words and phrases and later to become a storyteller too.

And, of course, the best stories to tell our children are stories about us when we were young.

The Way to Discover Books —
A Child Tells Us How We Can Help

When I'm Given a Book:
AT FIRST, by myself, I will:

- chew it
- throw it
- bang it
- tear it
- squeeze it
- look at the outside cover
- make sounds

And with a little help from you, I will:
- open and close it
- look at the pictures as the pages are turned
- feel what's on the page
- listen to your voice
- hear you imitate the sounds I make
- react to noises the book makes

THEN, by myself, I will:

- keep on chewing (Those cardboard ones are delicious!)
- throw, bang, tear, push the books across the floor, pull them off the shelf
- open and close a book
- look briefly at pictures
- recognize clear and simple pictures or photographs which remind me of my favorite people, animals, toys, food
- let you know that I want a story by dropping a book near you

And, with your help, I will:
- turn the pages, if you help me get started
- tap a page or try to grab the book
- follow your pointing finger or gestures
- get excited about a picture hidden under a flap — or on the next page when you turn the page slowly
- listen to the words and noises you make which relate to the pictures
- imitate the gestures or sounds you make if I've made them first
- concentrate only on the book and not look at you as well
- try to find the book if I see you hide it under a blanket

LATER, I will:

- chew less and turn pages more
- sit for a while and look at books myself
- put them back on the shelves (Can you believe it?)
- recognize my favorite book and get it off the shelf
- bring a book to you or try to climb on your lap and show you that I want a story

      And, with your help, I will:

- get a "book"
- follow your pointing finger and instruction to "Look!"
- point to familiar pictures and then look at you as if to say "What's that?" or "Hey, I recognize that!"
- imitate new easy sounds
- turn the pages when you get me started
- look for something hidden in the book
- imitate you when you touch something in the book
- enjoy books with a recurring theme
- enjoy books with flaps, pockets, and things that pop up

STILL LATER, I will:

- not chew, throw or bang
- choose my favorite book off the shelf, or go look for it
- look at it by myself
- point and vocalize to myself
- bring a book to you

      And, with your help, I will:

- find a specific book
- use a word or gesture to tell you which book I want to read
- turn pages
- fill in a sound or word or make a gesture when it's "my turn"
- point to pictures
- connect pictures in the book with real life
- enjoy stories which have a theme or a central character and a sequence of events.

Book List

Resource books for parents:

These books provide the parent with ideas and suggestions for rhymes, fingerplays and bouncing games to use with the child.

Beck, Ian	**Ride a Cock-Horse** (knee-jogging rhymes, patting songs and lullabies)
Briggs, Raymond	**Mother Goose Treasury**
Cole, Joanna	**The Eentsy, Weentsy Spider**
Glazer, Tom	**Eye Winker, Tom Tinker & Chin Chopper** (musical fingerplays)
King, Karen	**Oranges & Lemons** (singing & dancing games)
Matterson, Elizabeth	**This Little Puffin**
Williams, Sarah	**Round and Round the Garden**

Books to use with your child:

At first

Baer, Gene	**Thump, Thump Rat-a-Tat-Tat**
Bruna, Dick	**B is for Bear**
	I Can Count
	I Can Count More
	Word Book
	All My Toys
Campbell, Rod	**Dear Zoo**
Crowther, Robert	**The Most Amazing Hide-and-Seek Alphabet Book**
Gretz, Susanna	**Teddybears ABC**
	Teddybears 1 to 10
Hill, Eric	**Spot's 1st Book of Words**
Hoban, Tana	**1,2,3**
	Red, Yellow, Blue
	What is it? (board)
Kuskin, Karla	**Roar and More**
Look at Me	**Bathtime; Look at Me; Mealtime; Playtime** (board)
Look Baby Books	**Animal Friends; Favorite Things; My Busy Day; Time for Play** (board)
Oxenbury, Helen	**Dressing; Family; Friends; Playing; Working; Beach Day; Good Night, Good Morning;**

	Mother's Helper; Monkey See, Monkey Do; Shopping Trip (board)
Real Mother Goose	**Red Husky Book**
	Green Husky Book
	Blue Husky Book
	Yellow Husky Book (board)
Salt, Jane	**First Words**
Thompson, Brian	**Puffin First Picture Dictionary**
Wildsmith, Brian	**ABC**
	Mother Goose

This is a good time for homemade books with pictures of objects especially interesting to the child cut from magazines and glued to heavy scrapbook pages. Photos of family members, pets and home are also good and help the development of naming.

Then

Berger, Terry	**Ben's ABC Day**	Jam, Teddy	**Night Cars**
Blake, Quentin	**Mister Magnolia**	Langstaff, John	**Over in the Meadow**
Bodger, Joan	**Belinda's Ball**	Martin, Bill	**Brown Bear Brown Bear What do You See?**
Boynton, Sandra	**But Not the Hippopotamus**		
	The Going to Bed Book		**Polar Bear Polar Bear What do You Hear?**
	Moo Baa La La La		
	Opposites (board)		**My First Look At Time; Home;**
Brooke, Leslie	**Rhymes from Ring O'Roses**		**Nature; Sizes; Things that go;**
Brown, Margaret	**Goodnight Moon**		**Counting**
Burningham, John	**The Baby; The Blanket; The**	Rey, H.L.	**Anybody at Home?**
	Cupboard; The Dog; The Friend;		**Where's My Baby?**
	The Rabbit; The School; The Snow	Scarry, Richard	**The Best Word Book Ever**
Carle, Eric	**Do You Want to Be My Friend?**	Seuss, Dr.	**The Cat in the Hat**
	The Very Hungry Caterpillar		**The Cat in the Hat Comes Back**
de Paola, Tomi	**The Friendly Beasts**		**One Fish Two Fish Red Fish**
	(a Christmas story)		**Blue Fish**
Eastman, Phillip	**Go Dog Go**	Spier, Peter	**Crash! Bang! Boom!**
Falwell, Cathryn	**Where's Nicky?**		**Fast Slow, High Low**
Fleming, Denise	**In the Tall Tall Grass**		**Gobble, Growl, Grunt**
Gag, Wanda	**The ABC Bunny**	Stinson, Kathy	**Red is Best**
Garland, Sarah	**All Gone**	Weiss, Nicki	**Where Does the Brown Bear Go?**
Hoban, Tana	**Is it Red? Is it Yellow?**	Williams, Sue	**I Went Walking**
	Is it Blue?	Williams, Vera	**More More More Said the Baby**
	Round & Round & Round	Wildsmith, Brian	**The Cat on the Mat**
			The Circus
		Zacharias, Thomas & Wanda	**But Where is the Green Parrot?**

Later

Ahlberg, Janet & Allan	**Each Peach Pear Plum**	Ets, Marie Hall	**In the Forest**
			Play With Me
Allen, Pamela	**Fancy That!**	Flack, Marjorie	**Ask Mr. Bear**
Aliki	**Hush Little Baby**		**Angus and the Cats**
Bemelmans, Ludwig	**Madeline**		**Angus and the Ducks**
Brown, Marcia	**Three Billy Goats Gruff**		**Angus Lost**
Burningham, John	**Mr. Gumpy's Outing**	Fox, Mem	**Hattie and the Fox**
	Mr. Gumpy's Motor Car	Gag, Wanda	**Millions of Cats**
Chase, Edith N.	**The New Baby Calf**	Galdone, Paul	**The Little Red Hen**
Chorao, Kay	**Kate's Box; Kate's Car**		**The Three Bears**
Crews, Donald	**Freight Train**	Gibson, Betty	**The Story of Little Quack**
	Harbor	Ginsburg, Mira	**Across the Stream**
	Parade		**Good Morning Chick**
			Three Kittens
Dabcovich, Lydia	**Sleepy Bear**	Hennessy, B.G.	**Jake Baked a Cake**
Dodds, Dayle Ann	**Wheel Away!**	Hill, Eric	**Where's Spot?**
Ehlert, Lois	**Planting A Rainbow**		**Spot's First Walk**
Emberley, Barbara and Ed	**Drummer Hoff**		**Spot's Birthday Party**
		Hutchins, Pat	**Rosie's Walk**
			You'll Soon Grow Into Them Titch

Keats, Ezra Jack	**The Snowy Day**	Petersham, Maud & Mika	**The Box With the Red Wheels**
Krauss, Ruth	**The Happy Day**		
Langstaff, John	**Over in the Meadow**	Rice, Eve	**Oh Lewis**
Lottridge, Celia	**One Watermelon Seed**		**Sam Who Never Forgets**
Murphy, Jill	**Peace At Last**	Robart, Rose	**The Cake That Mack Ate**
nichol, bp	**Once: A Lullaby**	Sutton, Eve	**My Cat Likes to Hide in Boxes**
Oppenheim, Joanne	**Have You Seen Birds?**	Vipont, Elfrida	**The Elephant and the Bad Baby**
Oxenbury, Helen	**Bill and Stanley**	Watanabe, Shigo	**How Do I Put it On?**
	The Great Big Enormous Turnip	Zelinsky, Paul	**The Wheels on the Bus** (pop-up)

Still later

Anno, Mitsumasa	**Anno's Counting Book**	Lobel, Arnold	**Frog and Toad are Friends**
Baker, Keith	**Who is the Beast?**		**Frog and Toad Together**
Barton, Byron	**Airport**		**Owl at Home**
Bennett, Jill	**Tiny Tim, Verses for Children**	McCloskey, Robert	**Blueberries for Sal**
Burton, Virginia Lee	**Katy and the Big Snow**		**Make Way for Ducklings**
	The Little House	Milne, A.A.	**When We Were Very Young**
	Mike Mulligan and His Steam Shovel		**Now We Are Six**
		Minarik, Elsie	**Little Bear**
de Regniers, Beatrice Shenk	**May I Bring A Friend**		**A Kiss For Little Bear**
		Mollel, Tololwa	**Rhinos for Lunch and Elephants for Supper!**
Fox, Mem	**Shoes from Grandpa**		
Freeman, Don	**Corduroy**	Morgan, Allen	**Sadie and the Snowman**
Gilman, Phoebe	**Jillian Jiggs**	Rosen, Michael	**We're Going on a Bear Hunt**
Henkes, Kevin	**Sheila Rae the Brave**	Slobodkina, Esphyr	**Caps for Sale**
Hoberman, Mary Ann	**A House is a House for Me**	Waber, Bernard	**Ira Sleeps Over**
Hoban, Russell	**Bedtime for Frances**	Wells, Rosemary	**Benjamin and Tulip**
	A Birthday for Frances		**Noisy Nora**
Keats, Ezra Jack	**Whistle for Willie**	Williams, Linda	**The Little Old Lady Who Was Not Afraid of Anything**
Kerr, Judith	**Mog the Forgetful Cat**		
	Mog and the Baby	Zion, Gene	**Harry the Dirty Dog**
	The Tiger Who Came to Tea		**Harry by The Sea**
Krauss, Ruth	**The Carrot Seed**		**No Roses for Harry**
Leaf, Munro	**The Story of Ferdinand**		

The joys and benefits come from sharing the book, not from finishing the story quickly.

Stories to Tell

The Gingerbread Boy
Henny Penny
The Enormous Turnip
The Old Woman and Her Pig
The Travels of a Fox
The Frog and the Ox
Mommy Buy Me a China Doll (picture book by Margot Zemach)
The Little Red Hen
The Three Bears
The Three Billy Goats Gruff
The Three Little Pigs
The Name of the Tree (folktale retold by Celia Lottridge)

Most of the above stories (except the ones for which authors are given) can be found in the following collections of stories:

Chorao, Kay	**The Child's Fairy Tale Book**
Haviland, Virginia	**The Fairy Tale Treasury**
Oxenbury, Helen	**The Helen Oxenbury Nursery Story Book**
Rockwell, Ann	**The Three Bears and Fifteen Other Stories**
	The Three Sillies and Other Stories

CHAPTER EIGHT

Creating Together – Art

*"To create and share the creation is a way of communicating,
a way of sharing personal images."*

Frith Manolson, parent and art therapist

This chapter is about:

- the joy and benefit of helping our children create.

- being prepared so that we can create together as a natural part of our daily lives.

- how creating together opens new doors to conversation and learning.

- ideas for creative activities our children will enjoy.

Creating Together Leads to Communicating Together

The creative arts can be a non-threatening, undemanding place for us to connect and communicate with our children.

The nonverbal give and take of creating together, sharing supplies, exploring new materials, and working side by side leads naturally to verbal conversation.

In the process of creating, our children can express themselves without words. They let us know what interests them, how they perceive the world around them, and even how they are feeling.

We can learn so much about our children, and they can learn so much from us when we:

allow them to create in their own way

adapt our behaviour to share these special times with them; and

add information that will help them learn.

"The art of young children is a celebration of creativity, imagination and self-expression. Each creation reflects the uniqueness of the child who creates it, like a first step taken, a first word spoken."

Clare Cherry, education specialist

Making It Easy to Be Spontaneous

The key to getting started and having fun with art activities is having all the materials on hand, ready to use. Then, on a rainy afternoon, when we find we have an unexpected hour for playtime, out comes an old vinyl tablecloth to cover the floor, a box of paints, sheets of paper, dad's old shirt for a smock, and we're in business!

Surprisingly few materials are needed for creative activities.
Many of them can be found around our homes or workplace.

With a little imagination, something that was about to go out in the trash can become a key element in our child's work of art.

1. Don't throw away

Cardboard boxes of all sizes
Old sponges
Non-aerosol spray containers
Shampoo and liquid bath soap bottles
Paper towel/ toilet paper tubes
Fabric scraps
Sandpaper
Shirt cardboard
Newspapers and magazines
Paper bags
Mini raisin boxes
Old socks and gloves
Buttons
Coffee can lids
Macaroni

Empty spice containers
Food coloring
Shoe laces
Yarn
Empty spools of thread
Plastic yogurt containers
Baby food jars
Lids from frozen orange juice containers
Potatoes
Cotton swabs and balls
Old toothbrushes
Scraps of wrapping paper and ribbon
Shaving cream
Sand, leaves, rocks, twigs
Paper

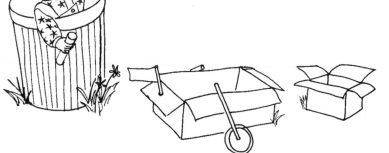

2. Gather up or go for

We may want to include additional items that are available from toy, hardware or art supply stores. Not all of these are necessary, but some are nice to have on hand. These include:

Crayons
Craypas (non-toxic oil-base pastels)
Tempera paint
Finger paint (see recipe below)
Felt-tip markers (non-toxic and washable)
Paint brushes
Sponge-tip brushes
Small paint rollers
Scissors
Glue sticks
White liquid glue
Colored tissue paper
Exacto knife (for adults only)
Masking and duct tape
Liquid acrylic

3. Paper

We use a lot of paper when we create art. Our children aren't fussy about what kind of paper we use; so used paper and envelopes are just fine, as are grocery bags, wallpaper, and newspaper. Another good source of paper is the local copy shop which often throws out scrap paper at the end of the day.

Ben's mom always had a roll of paper around — shelving paper, butcher block paper, or a roll of white paper she bought at an art store. She mounted it on the wall, on a dowel, like paper towel. In this way, Ben could let her know when he wanted to draw. At first he just liked to pull the paper and so she taped the roll shut and let him ask for it. Now that Ben is older and wiser, he uses the paper roll properly and often.

Having all materials on hand before getting started lets us stay fully focused on our child. Nothing disrupts creativity and sharing as much as having constantly to jump up and go off in search of new materials.

4. A place for everything

Keeping art material in one place — a shelf in the kitchen, laundry room or closet — makes it easier to start the fun of creating together.

Cardboard boxes, empty baby-wipe containers, plastic milk cartons (with the tops cut off and sharp edges taped) and empty cans of powdered infant formula make excellent storage containers. Use one for collage materials, one for fabric scraps and yarn and one for glues and glue-sticks, etc.

Taping a sample of what's inside a container onto the outside will make it easier for children to put things away where they belong. While this may sound like wishful thinking, since we will be the ones putting the supplies back for a while, our children will soon want to help. The effort to encourage good habits early eventually pays off.

5. Dress for the occasion

Art-making is an occasion when old shoes, old pants and old shirts are IN, and using masking tape or elastic to make them fit is fast and smart!

6. Set the stage

Nobody likes a mess! We can relax and enjoy the uninhibited and luxurious abandon of creating art with our children by taking a few minutes before we begin to cover the floor and table with newspaper, an old shower curtain or a vinyl tablecloth.

> **Tyler's Mom:** *"I found that an old plastic tablecloth or shower curtain attached to a pole or broom stick works wonderfully. I just roll it out when I need it and roll it back on the handle when I don't; when it gets too dirty, I just hose it off. I like leaving the pole rolled up against the wall because when Tyler wants to paint, he can let me know by pointing to the cloth."*

Keeping a sponge and paper towels near the work area makes wiping up spills easy, painless and fast.

Putting only small amounts of paint in containers that are heavy enough not to tip goes a long way toward preventing a mess from spilled paint. Using empty plastic squeeze bottles to store paint makes it easy to add paint as more is needed.

Communicating While Creating

1. Using the 3a Way

When we encourage our child to express himself nonverbally and acknowledge his efforts, it confirms for him our acceptance of his core being. Our positive responses support our child's true sense of self and the all-important feeling of self-esteem.

Young children often have a short attention span, and our exciting creative projects will be over in a few seconds unless we are there to help them explore the materials. When we first introduce materials, our participation is necessary. Once our children become involved, we can help them best by allowing them to lead and create in their own way.

> **Ben's Mom:** *"I was sure Ben would love to paint 'Happy Faces'. Every kid loves 'Happy Faces', but Ben had other ideas. He wanted to scribble. So I abandoned the 'Happy Faces' idea and followed Ben's lead. We had a great time together taking turns scribbling on the page. Where is it written that you have to make 'Happy Faces'?"*

Allow

When we ALLOW our children to lead, imitate what they are doing, or interpret what they are trying to tell us, it lets them know that they have our full attention; then when we pause and wait expectantly, they are encouraged to take their turn in conversation. Taking turns often begins when we imitate what our children do or say, when they roll the dough, crumple paper or put their hand in paint.

> **Laya's Dad:** *"Laya stuck her hand in the paint and so I stuck my hand in the paint too and made a hand print . And I said: 'Daddy's hand, Laya's hand'. We kept taking turns and soon a beautiful mural appeared."*

Each child is different. Some children complete a project quickly and want to start another. Others go at a slower pace and enjoy creating detail. Allowing our children to lead gives them the support and encouragement to create at their own pace.

Adapt

We can ADAPT the art activities so our children have something to communicate about.

Katie's Dad: *"We want to encourage Katie to use the words she knows and not just always point to things. When we made a face on paper by gluing the eyes, nose, mouth and ears on, it was a whole other way for her to experience and hear those words. Think of all the pictures we can draw together: Katie's activities, her school bus, her friends. The possibilities for language are just endless."*

We can create opportunities for our child to take the initiative in "sharing the moment" with us when we

- give him only one crayon or one paint color at a time
- give him a pencil that needs sharpening, scissors that don't cut
- keep extra materials in view but out of reach
- tighten the lid on the glue or paint jar

Add

When we ADD information by commenting on what our children are doing while they are creating, they hear the words that describe their actions and know we are interested in what they are doing — a good beginning for communication.

Tyler's Mom wanted to help him learn the word "up". So when she noticed Tyler making a mark on the paper, she followed and made a line with a circle on top and said, "Up, up balloon". Tyler copied, and they began to take turns. Tyler could see her hand moving up the page as it drew the line and hear the word "up" at the same time. "Up" then became an important word in other situations like "up the stairs", "want up" and "pick up".

2. Open-ended questions

Instead of...

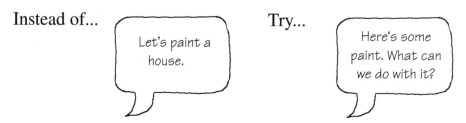

Let's paint a house.

Try...

Here's some paint. What can we do with it?

Open-ended questions can help get a dialogue going.

It is a mistake to assume that we know what our child's creation is all about. Something we may think is a drawing of a boot may, in our child's eye, be a polar bear. If we ask our child to tell us about it, rather than say what we think it is, we can learn a lot more about our child's thinking.

Katie drew something she said was a cat. Her mom asked questions that kept the drawing and the conversation going: "Where's the cat going?" "What is your cat doing?" "Does your cat have a friend?"

Like Katie's mom, we can encourage our children to respond by asking genuine questions, for example:

- What's happening now?
- Tell me about it.
- What's going on over there?
- What's going to happen next?
- What do you need?
- I see a yellow hand print. How do you do it?

Avoid test questions that ask information we already know — like "What colour is that?, How many is that?, What shape is that?".

What do you say to a work of art?

Jane's mom thought she was encouraging Jane by saying "that's wonderful" to everything Jane created. But then there was nothing more for Jane to say, and so the conversations ended. It is better to ask our child to tell us about her work or to describe what we see rather than to label or pass judgement. Remember, it's not what it looks like to us that matters; it's what it means to our child.

Cleaning up —
A chance for more fun and conversation

When we see that our child's interest or attention is flagging, it's time to start cleaning up. If we are running short of time and our child is still very much involved, we can help him make the transition to another activity by giving him a 5 minute warning and making clean-up a fun time.

Washing the brushes, putting the crayons in the hole of the tin, and cleaning stray crayon marks off a wall with a spray cleaner and paper towel (under our supervision) can be even more exciting than coloring.

To create a positive mood, so that clean-up doesn't become a chore but a time for more conversation and fun, we can:

- leave enough time for clean-up
- plan washing and putting away so they're fun to do
- acknowledge our child's efforts
- play some special music
- talk about what we're doing
- talk about what we'll do next

Our children benefit from helping in clean-up: they have the opportunity to learn by doing, they gain a sense of responsibility, and they learn that cleaning up is part of every activity.

Show it off for all to see and talk about

What refrigerator today is not covered with a constantly changing show of unique and special drawings? The final creation provides a visual record of the experience and can stimulate a lot of conversation. Our children's work can be made into books and albums; paintings can be covered with plastic and used as placemats. Masterpieces can be hung on walls, windows, and mirrors, preferably as low as possible so the artist can enjoy viewing his works of art with the rest of the family.

Putting up our children's artwork for friends and family to see shows we are proud of their accomplishments. Hearing others admire it builds their self-esteem and provides lots of happy opportunities to talk about it.

The Ability to Create —
How It Starts and Grows

AT FIRST ...sensory awareness and stimulation

— manipulates various objects and materials to explore texture, temperature, color, hardness, etc.

— attends to activity for brief amounts of time before being distracted

— imitates simple body actions while manipulating objects or art material

— enjoys simple games using art materials (e.g., putting clay in a bucket, hiding a brightly colored puppet and then finding it...)

THEN ... random and uncontrolled scribbling

— has no control of arm motion

— makes indiscriminate marks on drawing or modelling surface

— manipulating the object is of primary interest; has little interest in the motions made

— often babbles while using materials

— usually works very quickly

LATER ... controlled scribbling

— lines, color and forms take on specific meaning

— begins to control movements to create an overall pattern

— repetitive movements used to create patterns on surfaces

— can draw scribbles from left to right more easily than up and down

— patterns take on specific shapes; more control evident

— circle shape predominates in artwork

— child plans where he will draw

— symmetry and balance become important

— circle shape is divided into parts, or lines drawn on outside of circle go outward

LATER ...pre-representational drawing

— begins naming his art (e.g., calls a pattern of strokes "dog")

— draws simple human figures with arms and legs sticking out of head

— objects are not drawn standing on the ground (there is no groundline)

— objects are not drawn closer or farther away (e.g., objects are drawn all over the page, but not necessarily related to each other in size or location)

— trees and houses are attempted

— child is more interested in making shapes than in using appropriate colors

STILL LATER ... representational drawing

— begins to create what he is thinking

— work is unique and individualized

— groundline and skyline appear in drawings

— use of color is more realistic, reflecting its greater importance

Ideas for Creating Together

"The value of creating together is not the perfection or realism of the final product, but the sharing that takes place between parent and child during the process of creation. The things our child learns about her environment and capabilities, and what we learn about her are important benefits as well."

Susan Klein, parent and writer

At first

Your child may not be able to tell you what she is doing or how she feels, but if you allow her to lead she will certainly show you. Adapt to share the moment with her and add the language and experiences that will help her learn.

As your child explores new materials, you can share these experiences with her and help her discover other possibilities by mirroring her actions, expanding upon them and encouraging her to try others. A favourite activity like finger painting can be expanded on by mixing sand or shaving cream into paint. Talk to her about what you are doing.

Making your Mark

Place or tape (masking tape is easily removed) a large piece of paper onto the floor or tape it to a highchair tray. Give your child one crayon or marking pen at a time, naming the color. Craypas, which are oil-based pastels, are softer than crayons, and may be easier for a toddler to make marks with. Show your child how to mark the paper. When he makes a dot, line or other figure, mimic it. Encourage attempts at words by talking about colors and hand motions, and repeating any sounds or words he makes. Painting newspapers with water, using old paintbrushes or shaving brushes or fingers, is also a fun way to make marks.

Finger Painting

Finger paint is a wonderful way for children to see, to feel, and to explore their hand, arm and body movements. Finger paint can be bought at art stores, or you can make your own:

— 3 tbs. sugar
— 1/2 cup cornstarch
— 2 cups cold water
— 1 tbs. dishwashing detergent (approx.)
— food coloring

Mix all ingredients except food colouring and detergent.
Stir over low heat until mixture thickens and turns glossy.
Add about 1 tablespoon detergent and separate into containers
(baby food jars are excellent containers for this). Add food
coloring to the containers as desired.

Coated or glossy paper is best for finger painting because the paint won't soak into the paper and can easily be "swished" around. Coated paper can be bought at toy stores. Shelving paper also makes a great finger painting surface.

Put a small amount of one to two colors on the paper and show your child how to move it around with fingers and palms. Or you can start with footprinting. Lay the paper on the floor, and you and your child can step in the paint and then walk on the paper.

Shaving-Cream Portraits

You can have fun in front of the bathroom mirror. Help your child make marks with shaving cream; you can give yourselves beards, mustaches, head-dresses, or simply make squiggles on the mirror.

An alternative is to play hide-and-seek by having your child cover his reflection with shaving cream, and then ask "Where's Ben?" Help your child clean the shaving cream off the mirror with water and ask "Who's that?"

Keep a spray bottle filled with water and a sponge on hand for cleaning the mirror. A towel below the mirror makes for easier clean-up.

Then

As your child progresses, more physical control of materials becomes evident. Lines, color and forms take on specific meanings. Movements are repetitive. She can create an overall pattern that takes on a specific shape. If she is drawing or painting, she will plan where she will mark the paper.

Here are some projects that are appropriate at this stage:

Play Dough

The endless possibilities of play dough for experiencing change in shape, color, size and texture make it a great material for creating anything. To start off, just exploring the play dough is intriguing. Then it can be shaped into simple animals like snakes, turtles and alligators. Later, you can use cookie cutters to press shapes in the play dough. The cookie cutter shapes can be dried and painted with tempera and then a coat of acrylic.

Here is an especially good recipe for homemade play dough:

- — 3 cups white flour
- — 3 cups water
- — 2 tablespoons cream of tartar
- — 2 cups salt
- — 2 tablespoons oil
- — food coloring

Mix all dry ingredients in a large pot. Add water and oil. Mix well. Add food coloring and mix again. Cook over medium-high heat, stirring constantly until very firm and hot. Roll out on a floured board or table; fold and knead (like bread dough) to the proper consistency. Store in an airtight container.

Print Making with Homemade Stamps

Stamps can be small, everyday objects from around the house. Kitchen utensils, straws, cups, film cannisters, sponges, vegetables, leftover lids and old toothbrushes make excellent stamps.

Gather stamps and paper, and pour a little tempera onto paper plates. Dip the object into the paint so the bottom surface is coated. Press the object down on the paper, and then lift it up to discover the interesting print. Once your child masters the basic motions of stamping, you can use the shapes to create pictures of animals, vehicles, people, etc.

Take Chalk for a Walk

Next time you and your child go for a walk, bring along a stick of chalk and a spray bottle filled with water for erasing after yourselves. Draw figures on the sidewalk, and stand outside of them or within. Draw a circle in one spot and a square further down the side walk; then run back and forth between them. Take turns drawing shapes or simply squiggles.

A walk can be a lot of fun; an opportunity to create new images, enjoy new experiences and have conversations with your child.

Later

As your child's motor skills and eye-hand coordination progress, he will use materials in new ways. His creations take on meaning for him. A pattern of strokes becomes a dog or a blob of play dough is a penguin. It doesn't matter to the child that the blob doesn't look like a penguin, just that he knows it is one. He will try to draw simple human figures, trees and houses. He is more interested in making different shapes than in using appropriate colors.

Puppets

Towels, old socks, paper bags and small boxes can easily be transformed into puppets. The magic of puppets encourages children to express feelings they might not otherwise be able to express. For example, a child who pretends two puppet "children" are fighting may be showing his concern about an overly aggressive playmate.

By using a pen to mark eyes and a mouth, you can transform a paper bag into a puppet to while away time waiting at a grocery store check-out counter.

Two snack-size (1/2 oz.) raisin boxes make wonderful puppets for small fingers. Your child can paint the puppet, or he can cover it with colored paper using a glue stick. Use buttons for eyes, macaroni or cotton balls for hair, and felt for a tongue. Ask your child what the puppet should be, what color he should be painted, what materials he would like to use for hair, etc.

Spice Jar Rattle

Collect small objects from around the house or neighbourhood, such as buttons, nuts, bolts, pebbles, dry noodles, flower petals, beans and rice. Show your child how to drop the objects in an empty spice jar, describing each of them. This is an excellent activity for improving eye-hand coordination and learning about categories. Tape the lid securely shut and we have a wonderful rattle and display case for small treasures!

Cheerios Necklace

Making an edible necklace by stringing Cheerios onto a shoestring is an activity that can be done just about anywhere — at breakfast or while waiting at a doctor's office. It is also excellent for developing motor control and eye-hand coordination. Show your child how to string Cheerios, talk about the hole in the middle and how they look strung together.

Collages

Collage making is a great way to introduce your child to new textures, shapes and colors. It also provides opportunities for manipulating different kinds of objects.

Make a clear collage by assembling a variety of objects — buttons, tissue paper, leaves, twigs, flower petals, etc. — and clear sticky-back paper, sometimes known as contact paper. (It can be found in hardware and variety stores.) Roll out a large sheet, peel the backing off part of it, and arrange the objects on top of it. Talk with your child about the objects you are using, what they feel like, how they are shaped, and where he wants to put them. When you are finished arranging, peel the backing off the rest of the sheet, double it over and press it down.

For a "feelie" collage, assemble objects that have interesting textures, such as sandpaper, foil, felt, twigs, etc. Glue the objects on a sheet of paper, describing each as you go.

For a variation on "peek-a-boo", glue a scrap of fabric over a small mirror and watch your child's reaction when he sees your face or his own in the mirror.

Still later

Your child will begin to create what he is thinking, and his creations will begin to match reality. Painted lions are yellow. Groundline and skyline will appear in drawings, and the use of color will be more realistic, reflecting its greater importance to the child. Your child will also be able to communicate his feelings through his artwork.

Cardboard Vehicles and Structures

You can build an entire village with your child out of cardboard boxes salvaged from a trash bin. For larger structures, such as playhouses, fire stations, airplane hangars, etc., look for giant cardboard boxes in trash bins behind appliance and furniture stores. Use smaller boxes to make stoves, kitchen sinks, taxis, buses, trains, rowboats. Here are directions for a play-house to get you started, but you don't need to stop here. With imagination and cardboard, there's no limit to what you can make.

To make a playhouse, use an exacto knife to cut out windows and doors. Be careful not to let your child near the knife. Ask him to show you where he wants windows and doors, and what size and shape they should be. Use a large ruler and pencil to ensure lines to be cut are straight. Encourage your child to hold the ruler and/or draw the pencil line. Once the knife is out of reach, your child can get fully involved in this project. Paint the house with tempera. (For a sturdier, brighter finish, we can give it a primer coat ourselves with water-base house paint.) Ask your child what colors he would like to paint the house, doors, shutters, etc. Then turn him loose with a paint brush.

Search the garage or hardware store sales for drawer pulls to use as doorknobs. Help your child insert them with a bolt. (Tip: Use a leftover small square of cardboard as a washer.)

Don't worry if your child wants to paint the house a wild color or the painting job looks patchy. It's his house and he will love it all the more if it is the way he wants it.

Photo Album Books

Pick an event that is of special importance to your child: a journey to visit grandparents, a trip to the zoo, or even a ride on the bus to the grocery store. Bring along a camera and take lots of pictures of your child and the things that most interest her.

Put the photographs in a small photo album, skipping every other page. Then get ready to write (or take dictation for) your child's first book. Cut out paper to fit the blank pages. Sit down with your child and ask her what she would like to say about each photograph, and write it down or draw rough sketches.

Photo album books are a wonderful way for children to gain a sense of recording their experiences. The albums provide limitless opportunities for conversation.

In Conclusion

Helping our children learn to communicate isn't as straightforward as baking a cake or building a bookshelf. There's no sure-fire, never-fail method. How we encourage communication varies with each individual child.

What we've been discussing are basic guidelines, and with practice, we'll find the "recipe" that works best for our child. We'll discover what he responds to and what he turns away from, what helps him learn and what doesn't.

We'll learn to trust our instincts. But when our instincts need a little help, we can remember to **OWL** ...and use the **3a** approach.

Observe  **a**llow our child to lead us

Wait and **a**dapt to share the moment

Listen **a**dd language and experience

The Prince Who Would Be A Rooster: A 3a Way Folktale

*This ancient folktale reminds us of the value of the **3a** approach, in connecting with a child to help him learn (**a**llow the child to lead, **a**dapt to share the experience, and **a**dd Information).*

Once upon a time, many years ago, in a small kingdom far away, there lived a King, a Queen and their only child, the young prince. In the eyes of the King and Queen, the sun rose and set for their darling boy. They made sure that he had the most famous of teachers and the wisest of soothsayers to instruct him for his future role of king.

One day, a terrible thing happened...the prince removed his royal robes and wandered through the castle flapping his arms and crowing like a rooster! He wouldn't eat with the King and Queen, only eating corn off the floor.

The King and Queen were very, very upset. They sent for the best doctors in the kingdom. Some doctors tried pills and potions, others tried magic and incantation, but all to no avail. The rooster prince still crowed and flapped happily around the castle. The King and Queen were in despair.

One fine morning a wise old man with a long, white beard and twinkling, blue eyes presented himself at the castle and said: "Your royal highnesses, I'm sure I can cure the prince." "But where are your medicines?" inquired the King with surprise. "I have my own way, your majesty," replied the old man, "but I must have seven days alone with the prince."

The King and Queen, though skeptical, granted the wise man's request. The wise man was left alone with the prince. He first removed all his clothes, then he crouched next to the rooster prince and began to flap his arms. Carefully the prince studied his new companion. "Who are you?" crowed the rooster prince inquisitively. "I am a rooster, can't you tell?" said the wise man gently. "How wonderful, I am a rooster too!" answered the prince, so pleased to have a new friend.

The two rooster companions happily flapped and crowed their way around the castle. Then slowly, the old man began to straighten up as he walked. The rooster prince, wanting to stay close to his friend, stood a little straighter. The next day, the old man put on his trousers and a clean shirt.

"What's that you have on?" questioned the prince. "Roosters don't wear clothes!" "You are right, my friend, but the castle is drafty and I was getting a bit cold. You can be a good rooster, even wearing clothes. Why don't you try it?" suggested the wise man.

The rooster prince dressed as his friend had done and together they continued happily crowing and flapping around the castle. The following morning, the old man sat at the table and ate grain from a silver dish. The rooster prince perched on a chair next to his friend. With a wink to the servants, the wise man had the table laid with silverware, goblets, platters and a tempting array of foods. The prince watched as the wise man used his utensils and drank from his goblet and soon began to do the same. The rooster prince crowed with real delight as he finished this feast. The next day, the old man started a philosophical discussion with the prince. "Just a minute," cried the prince, "roosters don't have to think. They are fed and looked after and crow and flap without any cares."

"You are right", replied the wise old man, "but a rooster can still be a good rooster even if he discusses the meaning of life."

The prince pondered this and began to discuss important issues with his friend. On the morning of the seventh day, the wise old man bid farewell to the prince. As he was leaving , he said "Remember, my friend, roosters are fair game for the hunter. If I were you I would pretend to be a prince. Rule wisely and do good deeds. Farewell, my friend."

From that moment on, the prince walked upright, ate, spoke and behaved in ways befitting a prince. And when the time came for him to rule over the kingdom he ruled wisely and well and no one but he had any idea that he was really a rooster.

A Record of How Your Child is Communicating Now

Keeping the following checklists will help you recognize how your child is now communicating and what the next steps will likely be.

• **A Getting-to-Dialogue Checklist** *of what your child does, says and understands to determine the level of communication development your child has reached.*

• **Three Communication-Observation Reports** *that focus on when, how, why and about what your child communicates.* (Adapted from Ecological Communication Organization by J.D. MacDonald and A. Iglesias)

• **A Speech Sounds Checklist, Vocabulary Checklist and Language Sample** *to record the sounds, words, signs or picture board symbols your child uses.*

Anything your child does to make his needs, wants and interests known is communication. This may be crying, whining, and gesturing, as well as sounds, words, phrases, or signs. Let's be sure to note them all. You may want to check with others who know your child well to see what their opinions are.

Getting-to-Dialogue Checklist

Please check (√) the statements below which best describe your child.

Level I: Child Responds Primarily on Reflex Basis

Child Does	Child Says	Child Understands
A. Responds only on reflex basis ___ May show startle response to sudden changes (noises, lights, movement) ___ Turns head towards a sound ___ Sucks on nipple ___ Briefly grasps object placed in hand	___ Cries and makes some throaty sounds	
B. Reacts to some people, objects or events ___ Looks at object placed in front of him ___ Follows movement with eyes and hands ___ Grasps and holds	___ Communicates immediate wants and needs by varying the manner in which he whines or cries – for example, crying to signal that he is hungry or in distress ___ Makes vowel-like sounds to express pleasure and displeasure (other than crying) ___ May vocalize when sounds are heard but does not directly imitate.	___ Responds differentially to various intonation patterns

Level II: Child Begins to Explore the Environment and Starts to Imitate Actions and Sounds

Child Does	Child Says	Child Understands
___ Reaches, creeps or crawls towards objects or people ___ Does the same action to different objects – for example, mouths everything ___ Imitates simple body actions he has initiated ___ Imitates simple body actions initiated by someone else ___ Attends to specific events and objects but is easily distracted	___ Enjoys making sounds ___ Shows interest in gaining and maintaining your attention ___ Makes sounds to accompany actions ___ Uses a variety of vowel and consonant combinations (e.g., ga-ga, ba-ba) ___ Imitates familiar sounds he has initiated ___ Imitates familiar sounds initiated by someone else	___ Appears to recognize gestures and a few words like "daddy", "up", "no", "bye-bye" and own name in context ___ Anticipates steps within daily routines – for example, gets excited when he sees food or water in bathtub

Level III: Child Begins to Communicate Using Conventional Sounds and Gestures

Child Does	Child Says	Child Understands
A. Coordinates sounds, gestures and eye contact		
___ Looks and/or uses some basic gestures to get attention	___ Communicates needs using crying and eye gazing with some gestures – for example, looking at you and holding out arms to be picked up	___ Follows some simple instructions – for example, "give a kiss", "wave bye-bye", "give it to me"
___ Looks to make direct eye contact		
___ Plays appropriately with some toys	___ Begins to use adult intonation in babbling	
___ Attends to activity/person for a longer period of time	___ Attempts to imitate new sounds	
___ Attempts to imitate new actions		
___ Begins to participate actively in games like "peek-a-boo", "pat-a-cake", "catch me", "toss away", and plays with pull toys		
___ Can request that games continue		
B. Shifts focus from object of interest to the person he is playing with, and back again		
___ Consistently points, tugs, touches, shows, gives, etc. to request objects and actions or to get attention	___ Uses voice in conjunction with pointing and gesturing to request objects and actions	___ Points to some body parts
		___ Identifies some familiar people and objects when named
___ May begin to express needs with consistent pantomime	___ Tries different sounds to reach a specific goal	___ Appears to understand simple requests when accompanied by your gestures or actions — for example, "throw the ball"
___ Tries different actions to reach a specific goal	___ May use 1-5 words — for example, "mama, dada"	
___ Fills turn in a familiar activity – for example, not only waits but does something to complete turn	___ Uses some exclamations like "oh-oh"	
___ Takes more than one turn in a taking-turns activity — for example, alternating with you in putting rings on a stick or blocks on top of each other	___ Frequently responds to songs or rhymes by vocalizing	
	___ Successfully imitates new sounds — for example, motors, animals	
___ Successfully imitates new actions		

Level IV: Child Begins to Communicate Using Words

Child Does	Child Says	Child Understands
___ Continues to communicate using gestures ___ Pretend behavior begins initially with self-pretend and then with objects ___ Imitates actions previously seen	___ Continues to use voice in conjunction with pointing and gesturing ___ Consistently uses a limited number of words — for example, "no", "there", "all gone", "up", "bye-bye" ___ Often uses only initial consonants and vowels	___ Understands about 50 words ___ Understands simple questions ___ Follows directions in familiar situations such as "sit down", "come here", "stop that"
Then: ___ Consistently uses a limited vocabulary	___ Generally uses single words to communicate ___ Answers "yes" and "no" questions ___ Responds to question "What's this?" with an object name	___ Understands words even when object is not present ___ Points to body parts and clothing shown in large pictures ___ Follows 2 step directions — for example, "Get me the ball. Throw it to Daddy."
___ Begins to combine words	___ Imitates some 2-3 word sentences ___ Sometimes spontaneously uses 2 word phrases ___ Uses some questions — "what?", "where?" ___ May have approximately 50 or more single words	___ Understands about 100 words ___ When asked, can select an object from larger group of objects
___ Usually uses 2 and 3 word phrases	___ Uses questions more often – "what?", "where?", "who?" ___ Uses negative form "no" substituted for "not"	___ Points to picture of familiar object described by its use — for example, "What do you eat with?" ___ Responds to "where?" questions ___ Understands about things in past and future
___ Continues to use longer and more complex sentences	___ Uses "why?", "when?", and "how?" questions ___ Uses more mature grammar	___ Understands prepositions such as "on", "under", "front", "behind"

Summary of Checklist

Review pages 137 to 139.

Please check (√)which **levels** best describes your child's abilities.

	To Do	To Say	To Understand
Level I: **Responds primarily on reflex basis**			
Level II: **Explores the environment and imitates**			
Level III: **Coordinates sounds, gestures and eye contact to communicate** **Can shift focus from object of interest to the person he is playing with and back again**			
Level IV: **Begins to use words**			

Knowing at what level your child is communicating now will help you help your child progress to the next level.

1. When Your Child Communicates

In this first communication-observation report, let's take a look at what your child does and who is with her during a "typical" weekday and weekend.

	Child's Weekday Activities	Who is directly involved?	Who else is around?
7:00 – 9:00			
9:00 – 12:00			
12:00 – 1:00			
1:00 – 3:00			
3:00 – 5:00			
5:00 –7:00			
7:00 – 9:00			
	Child's Weekend Activities		
Morning			
Afternoon			
Evening			

2: How and Why Your Child Communicates

You spend more time with your child and know him best and so your evaluation of his present communication skills is most valuable. Observe, listen to your child and try to be very accurate when filling out the following form.

In this second communication-observation report, please check (√) the columns below to show **how** and **why** your child usually communicates.

WHY your child communicates

HOW your child communicates	To protest	To request actions/objects	To get attention	To express feelings+interest	To imitate	To greet	To label or describe	To answer	To ask questions	To comment on what can't be seen
Level I										
Cries										
Smiles										
Screams										
Makes vowel-like sounds										
Looks										
Random arm or hand movements										
Level II										
Uses facial expressions										
Laughs										
Makes a variety of consonant and vowel sounds										
Reaches										
Level III										
Shakes head or nods										
Looks to make eye contact										
Points, gestures										
Pantomimes – acts out what he wants to say										
Uses sounds that stand for words										
Occasionally uses single words										
Level IV										
Frequently uses single words										
Combines words – hard to understand										
Combines two or more words										
Uses sign language or communication board										

3. What Your Child Communicates About

In this third communication-observation report, check how frequently your child communicates about each topic listed below and give an example. Remember, your child may communicate with body language, sounds, sign language, communication board or words.

HOW OFTEN your child communicates

Your child communicates ABOUT	Always	Usually	Sometimes	Never	Example
Food or drink					
Toys					
Clothes					
Pets					
Other things					
Parents					
Brothers and sisters					
Relatives					
Friends					
Neighbours					
Teacher					
Babysitter					
Other people					
Eating					
Toileting					
Playing					
Going for a ride					
TV					
Listening to music					
Other activities					

Summary of Communication-Observation Reports

1. When your child communicates

Each parent should complete this section independently.
For you and your child, there are some situations which
are better for communicating than others. Look at
page 141, and complete the form below.

When you now encourage communication	When you could encourage communication	When it is inappropriate to encourage communication

2. How and why your child communicates

Look at page 142. Circle the highest level (I-IV) your child has reached for each of the reasons listed below.

To protest..........Level   I   II   III   IV

To request actions/objects..........Level   I   II   III   IV

To get attention..........Level   I   II   III   IV

To express feelings and interest..........Level   I   II   III   IV

To imitate..........Level   I   II   III   IV

To greet..........Level   I   II   III   IV

To label and describe..........Level   I   II   III   IV

To answer..........Level   I   II   III   IV

To ask questions..........Level   I   II   III   IV

To comment on what can't be seen..........Level   I   II   III   IV

3. What your child communicates about

Look at page 143. Note what your child communicates about.

Always _____

Usually _____

Sometimes _____

Never _____

4. Vocabulary List

If your child uses gestures, sounds or simple words, use this sheet to record all her attempts to communicate.

Gesture, Sound or Word	Meaning

5. Speech Sounds Checklist

Some sounds are easier for your child to make than others. Please circle the sounds your child can make now.

Vowel Sounds

First: **ee** as in f*ee*t
  a as in f*a*ther
  oo as in wh*o*

Then: **aw** as in f*a*ll
  e as in g*e*t

Later: **ai** as in p*ie*
  au as in c*ow*
  oi as in t*oy*
  ei as in pl*ay*

Consonant Sounds

First: **p, b, m, n, w**
  t, d, k, g, h, ng (as in si*ng*)

Then: **f, s, l, y** (as in *y*ellow)
  sh (as in *sh*ip)
  v, z, r, ch (as in *ch*ew)
  dg (as in *j*uice)

Later: **th** (as in *th*ing)
  th (as in *th*is)
  s (as in mea*s*ure)

6. Language Sample

If your child uses **two or more** word phrases to communicate, record all his efforts here.

My Child Says and/or Does	My Child Means

Once is not enough. It's important to review periodically your child's progress to see how far he has come and what his next steps will be. This information will help you adapt to your child's changing abilities and your everchanging role in helping him progress.

Index

CHAPTER THREE — Add Language And Experience   33

CHAPTER FOUR: Play The 3a Way   55

CHAPTER SEVEN: Sharing Books   103

CHAPTER EIGHT: Creating Together — Art   117